Modern Dressmaking

A textbook for students

Gwyneth Watts

Hutchinson

London Melbourne Sydney Auckland Johannesburg

Hutchinson & Co. (Publishers) Ltd
An imprint of the Hutchinson Publishing Group
24 Highbury Crescent, London N5 1RX

Hutchinson Group (Australia) Pty Ltd
30-32 Cremorne Street, Richmond South, Victoria 3121
PO Box 151, Broadway, New South Wales 2007
Hutchinson Group (NZ) Ltd
32-34 View Road, PO Box 40-086, Glenfield, Auckland 10

Hutchinson Group (SA) (Pty) Ltd
PO Box 337, Bergvlei 2012, South Africa

First published 1981

© Gwyneth Watts 1981
Illustrations © Hutchinson & Co. (Publishers) Ltd 1981

Printed in Great Britain by The Anchor Press Ltd
and bound by Wm Brendon & Son Ltd, both of Tiptree, Essex

British Library Cataloguing in Publication Data
Watts, Gwyneth
    Modern dressmaking.
    1. Dressmaking
    I.   Title
    646.4'3'04   TT515

ISBN 0 09 143630 3 cased
        0 09 143631 1 paper

Contents

Preface

This book has been written to explain the necessary techniques as clearly as possible to assist the reader to develop the art of successful dressmaking.

Each chapter is preceded by stating the objectives. The final chapter consists of a number of multiple choice questions to use as a learning check for these objectives.

Fashions are constantly changing but the basic principles of garment construction remain the same, and this book is designed to serve as a permanent guide for practical application in the craft. Dressmaking is a creative art and modelling helps the student to develop this ability. Therefore, a chapter has been devoted to modelling a bodice and skirt on a dress stand. It is essential to experiment working in three dimensions, and thus to be able to practise the art of drapery and manipulation of fabric.

The subject matter of this book has been built up from experience gained in teaching the craft and also from my involvement as a visiting examiner and assessor for City and Guilds of London Institute. Although this book is intended for students preparing for examinations in City and Guilds Creative Studies Fashion Parts I and II, it will be a useful textbook for GCE Advanced level students. It should also be of considerable use to all dressmaking students.

I wish to take this opportunity of thanking my colleagues: Tricia Duffy for reading the text and Janette Thistlethwaite for typing the text.

Introduction

There are many things to consider when starting to make clothes. We all want to sew successfully; and to produce a pleasing, attractive result is very satisfying. The following chapters set out to show how to achieve such a result, dealing with each factor involved.

To plan a wardrobe which will cover all our needs, there are certain questions we must ask ourselves. Below are some of these:

What sort of life style do we have?
Do we wear more casual than formal clothes?
Do we spend most of our time with children?
Do we have many occasions to wear evening dress?

Careful planning will provide us with interchanges which will make our clothes more interesting. Basic garments such as skirts, trousers, tops, jackets can be changed round to give totally different effects. Accessories can be worn with basic garments to introduce other ideas. Style is an important factor which enables us to make the most of our figure type. In considering style, fabric will also be taken into account. Colour is important too. It can do much to enhance the overall image presented. Dressmaking is an art to enjoy, and working at it in detail will bring success.

Abbreviations

cm	centimetres
mm	millimetres
CF	centre front
CB	centre back
RS	right side
WS	wrong side
SS	side seam
RSS	right sides
WSS	wrong sides
×	by, e.g. length and width of crosswise strips
+	plus

part one

The Art – To Know How

chapter 1

Creative design for the dressmaker

After reading this chapter you will be able to:

1 Define the principles of design.

2 Develop an awareness of the points to be considered when selecting styles.

3 Establish the difference between creative design and drawing ability.

Creative design is a personal thing and just as people have different personalities, so do fabrics and colour. To make a garment successfully, fabric selection is important for it incorporates shade, texture and draping qualities. It will play a leading role in creating the silhouette of the garment.

When choosing a fabric hold it in the general lines of the style planned, and then ask these questions:

Does it fall into folds over the body curves?
Will it gather at the waist?
Will it give a crisp line to pleats?
Will it give a smooth or bulky appearance?
Will it respond to panel seaming?
Will it reflect an attractive shade under artificial lighting?

These are some of the things that will give guidance as to how a fabric will behave when being made up and when being worn. Wrong selection could give a disappointing result. The style must enhance the natural characteristics of the fabric, for example, soft style lines for soft fabrics. Never try to stiffen a soft fabric to give a crisp line or the natural softness will be lost.

The overall effect must be studied. Large figure types must avoid bulky fabrics which will add to size. Fabrics with a smooth, shiny surface which reflect light will also give an appearance of a larger figure. Tall, slender figure types must avoid too bulky or heavy fabrics, which may overpower the figure, and should select a fabric which will drape to give a softly curved line. If the figure is tall and too thin, add roundness by avoiding clinging fabrics which will show the thinness of the figure. If the figure is tall and heavily built, select a smooth texture with a matt surface, avoiding large patterned fabrics.

The short, slender figure must avoid overpowering the figure with coarse, heavy fabrics and fabrics with large pattern design. Soft fabrics and small patterned fabrics will enhance delicacy of the figure. If the figure is short and plump, heavy, coarse and shiny fabrics must be avoided. Soft fabrics, medium to light-weight, with a matt surface lend themselves to advantage to this figure type.

Style, figure and fabric must be considered together. Figure 1 (page 14) will give guidance in selecting correctly.

Having decided upon the fabric, consideration of colour is very important as this will be noticed first. Some colours drain the colour away from certain complexions. It is a good idea to hold the fabric from the neck line in front of the figure standing before a full length mirror. The image presented will give a very good idea as to whether a colour is suitable or not. It is possible to wear a colour successfully if another colour is added around the neck area, for example, a blouse with an overdress or a scarf worn at the neck line.

Blues/greens are cool, receding colours. Reds/oranges are advancing colours. Strong shades of advancing colours will make the figure appear larger.

The overall shape is the next consideration. This must be selected according to figure type and the image a fashionable woman is aiming to achieve. Structural style lines also play a part and should enhance the silhouette.

Figure type	Fabric	Style lines
Tall: slim/thin	Light to medium-weight, some surface texture.	Seaming across the figure. Soft rounded lines to avoid angular look. Soft drapes.
Tall: heavy build	Light to medium-weight, firm fabrics.	Tailored lines to give smooth effect. Panel seams.
Short: slim/petite	Soft, light to medium-weight. Small patterned fabrics.	Soft flowing lines, vertical seams, not too full to overpower the figure.
Short: plump	Light to medium-weight, matt surfaced.	Vertical seams, tailored lines to give height and take away plumpness.
Low busted	Light to medium-weight.	Gathers falling softly from yoke line. Upward curved empire line. French dart to give length to waist/bust measurement.
Flat chested	Soft, light to medium-weight. Good draping qualities.	Add measurement to bust line, horizontal lines. Empire line, softly gathered bodice. Cowl neck lines giving folds across front bodice.
Large hips	Smooth. Light to medium-weight for skirts and trousers.	A-line to flare slightly over the hips giving less emphasis to large hip area. Panel seams.
Short neck	Avoid rough textures and bulky fabrics around the neck area.	V-necks and open collars add length. Avoid high, round neck lines.

Figure 1

Horizontal lines add width, for example, waist-bands, jacket hem lines, horizontal pockets. Vertical lines add length, for example, princess seaming. As in colour, contrast in texture can help to balance a figure. A combination of shiny and matt surface fabrics will reduce and, at the same time, add width or length to an overall shape. Certain fabrics of bulky textures often make the figure appear smaller, especially if the fabrics are of receding colours.

Correct balance is achieved by considering together overall shape, style lines, colour and texture.

Creating designs

Develop the art of creating styles suitable to the fabric and the occasion for which the garment will be worn. Prepare and keep a folder for useful information and ideas for future use, for example, pockets, collars, decoration on garments. Study the work of designers and observe possible reasons for the success or failure of designs.

Observation, practice and experience help to build a certain amount of creativity. Fashion drawing is a very useful aid in helping to develop ideas and also in improving the skill of recording ideas in a sketch. The following suggestions will help those with no previous knowledge of drawing to produce a good working sketch, but regular practice is essential.

Use of templates

Basic figure templates are printed (Figure 212, page 119), and these may be used to form a basis for initial practice. Trace off the template and make a card outline to use. As confidence grows and experience increases, use extra templates of different

crisp

soft

for short
plump figure
types

for tall, slim
figure with
low bust line

for flat chest
and large hips

Figure 2   *Working drawings*

poses, for example, formal evening dress on standing figure, sportswear on running figure. Templates help to give correct proportions for the figure to produce good working drawings.

It is accepted that there are two types of fashion drawing:

1 *Fashion illustration* Artist's impression of a garment which is attractive enough to encourage people to choose the garment.
2 *Working drawing* An accurate record having every item clearly marked, for example, zips, pockets, flaps. A front and back view and at times, a side view are essential.

Drawing the garments

Garments of flimsy fabrics or of close fitting styles will follow the lines of the body shape. Outer garments and those of heavy fabrics will add bulk to the body shape. Soft fabrics will fall in folds while firm fabrics will hang in straight lines. The following list corresponds to numbers 1–8 on Figure 2.

1 Set-in sleeves are the only ones to have the underarm sleeve line drawn right up to the underarm point.
2 Other sleeve styles join the bodice much lower down, almost to the waist line in some cases. They are formed in a curved shape.
3 *Always* work on front and back views together, for example, draw front collar and back collar, CF waist line and CB waist line.
4 Fastenings on single-breasted garments sit on CF line.
5 Pockets, panel seams are equal distance from CF (not the jacket edge).
6 Collars meet at CF or CB.
7 Zips must be set into a seam line; the zip teeth are not usually seen.
8 Shaping to the body is shown by darts or seams. Place accordingly in correct positions.

Texture of fabric is shown by using different mediums, for example, brush/ink for silky texture.

Lightly draw the silhouette first, then the details of the style. Practise these techniques by using a basic dress design. To this add any creative ideas that come to mind to bring individuality to the style.

chapter 2

Understanding figure types

After reading this chapter you will be able to:

1   Assess different figure types.

2   Measure the figure correctly.

When choosing styles for garments, the points discussed in Chapter 1 must be taken into consideration. The overall image presented is important, and when choosing clothes to enhance certain figures, it is a good idea to look at different figure types so that the correct choice can be made.

The average figure is one that is not often seen, and most of us have some figure problem which can be easily overcome by careful choice of clothes.

To determine a figure type, measure and observe the silhouette of the figure and fit it into one of the following figure descriptions. Take the back neck to waist measurement and the overall height of the wearer; then study the details of what to look for in each figure type. The pattern size is determined by the body measurements.

Tall and slender The CB to waist measurement is usually longer than given on standard commercial patterns. Take this measurement accurately as a short waist position will give an amateur look to a garment and is not comfortable to wear.

Tall and thin The figure type is usually flat chested, has bony hips and is flat across the buttocks. Long CB to waist measurement.

Tall, heavily built This figure has a broad back and full bust measurement, long CB to waist and usually a large upper arm measurement.

Short, medium build Usually short waisted. Take the CB neck to waist measurement accurately as a too long waisted position will look dowdy.

Short and plump Usually short waisted. Check the CB neck to waist measurement to position the waist correctly. Usually a large upper arm, full bust and full abdomen measurements.

Low bust figure Measure carefully the underarm to waist area. As the bust level is low, measure the position of darts carefully and alter the pattern before cutting out the garment.

Measuring the figure

Remove any jacket or cardigan being worn and measure over a simple, well-fitting garment with set-in sleeves. The correct foundation garments should be worn. Tie a stay tape around the waist firmly to determine the natural waist line. Correct posture is important. Stand naturally, not stiffly; do not slouch or lean to one side as this will give an inaccurate measurement. The tape measure should be held firmly over the figure but not pulled tightly.

Order of measurement
Numbers 1–12 of the following list correspond to the numbers shown on Figure 3 (page 18).

1   *Bust* Measure closely around the fullest part of the figure, keeping the tape level.

2   *Waist* Along the natural waist line determined by the stay tape.

3   *Hips* 18–20 cm below the waist line over the fullest part of the figure.

4   *Back bodice length* Taken from the prominent bone at the base of the neck to the centre back of the waist.

Note: These four measurements must be taken to determine the correct pattern size required. The following list of measurements must be taken to be able to make the personal fitting of the pattern.

5   *Chest width* Halfway between the shoulder and the bust line across the chest from armhole seam.

6   *Back width* 10 cm down from the nape of the neck straight across the back over the shoulder blades.

7   *Shoulder* From neck to shoulder bone (check with armhole seam).

8   *Underarm length* Take this measurement with the arm extended outwards from the lowest point of the armhole to the wristbone.

9   *Outer arm length* Over the elbow with the arm slightly bent, from just below the shoulder, to the wrist bone. Take that measurement carefully to determine the exact position of the elbow dart.

10 *Upper arm* Around the top of the arm 8-10 cm below the shoulder. Right hand person measure right arm; left hand person measure left arm. This is because continual use can develop the upper arm and increase measurement.

Figure 3

11   *Wrist*   Over the wristbone – not too tightly.
12   *Skirt length*   From CB waist to hem line. For a full figure, measure at CF and side seam also. Measurements 4 plus 12 give CB neck to hem length.

Trousers

13   *Waist*   As measurement no. 2.
14   *Hip*   As measurement no. 3.
15   *Outside leg*   Waist to ankle. It is essential to wear correct shoes for this measurement so that the heel height may be considered (see Figure 4).

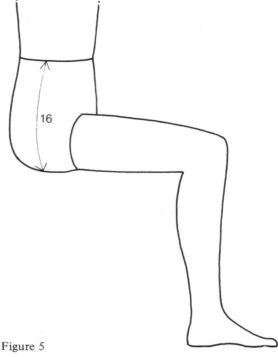

Figure 5

16   *Crotch depth*   This measurement is taken in a sitting position from the waist along the body curve to the chair seat. Add on 2–3 cm ease for a fuller figure type (see Figure 5).
17   *Inside leg*   Measurement no. 15 minus no. 16 will give this measurement.
18   *Thigh*   Take this measurement over the fullest part. Do not hold the tape tightly.

All these measurements are necessary regardless of the style of the garment. Make a record of the measurements, and at regular intervals check to note any changes in the figure so that necessary adjustments can be made.

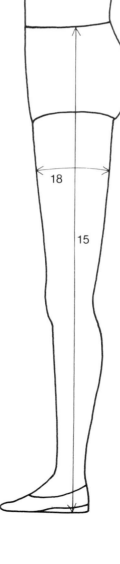

Figure 4

chapter 3

Alteration to patterns

After reading this chapter you will be able to:

1 Assess any alterations to be made to the pattern to give correct fitting.

2 Complete a finished pattern with the adjustments made and every symbol transferred correctly.

In Chapter 2 we looked at the understanding of figure types, how to size up and interpret the best style to enhance the silhouette. Fit is very important, and as patterns are made to the standard size, it is essential to know how to accommodate the pattern to fit a particular figure type. In order to do this we need to know the various figure problems which have to be dealt with and how to make the necessary alterations to the standard pattern.

When making alterations to a pattern the following points must be observed:

1 Keep to the original shape of the pattern piece as closely as possible so that the style of the garment is not distorted.

Figure 6   *To shorten*

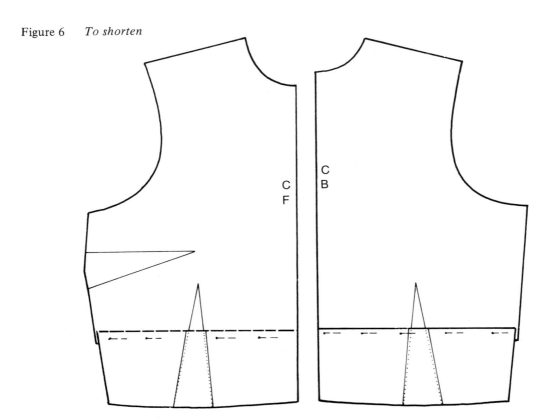

2 Any alteration must be made in an area which will not alter the shape of the pattern piece.
3 By careful measuring on each pattern piece, keep the 'straight of grain' running in the correct direction. To do this, extend the main part of the straight grain symbol.
4 Alterations must be accurate and must be made *before* the fabric is cut out.
5 Place new balance marks (notches) to match up each pattern piece in the construction of the garment to ensure correct balance and fit in the finished garment.

Most alterations are easily coped with and the following figures show how and where to make alterations.

Bodice alterations

Short waisted To shorten pattern, fold over the pattern as illustrated in Figure 6 for the amount required; pin fold in place.

Long waisted To lengthen pattern, cut the pattern as illustrated in Figure 7; spread for the amount required. Pin to a strip of paper placed underneath the pattern.

Round shoulders To prevent the bodice pulling across the shoulders, draw a straight line across the back bodice 10 cm below the CB neck (see Figure 8). Cut along this line, open up and raise the pattern for the amount needed. Pin to paper. Draw new CB line. Make a small neckline dart.

Erect back To remove any surplus amount of pattern, draw a straight line 10 cm below the CB neck to the armhole (see Figure 9). Fold out the amount required at CB, tapering to nothing at the armhole edge. Straighten the CB line.

Sloping shoulders Make the alteration to back and front armholes. Lower the shoulder line at the armhole edge (see Figure 10). Lower the same amount at the underarm to retain the size and shape of the original armhole.

Square shoulders Make the alterations to the

Figure 7
To lengthen

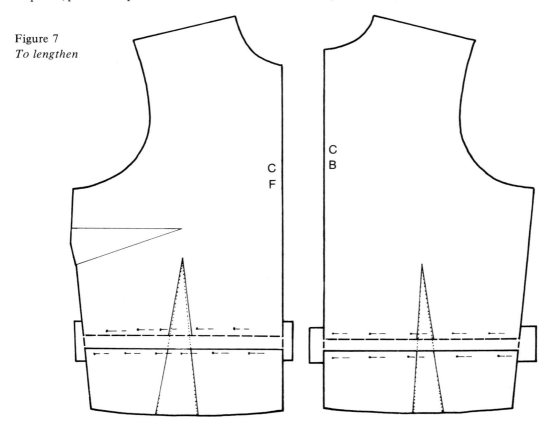

C F

C B

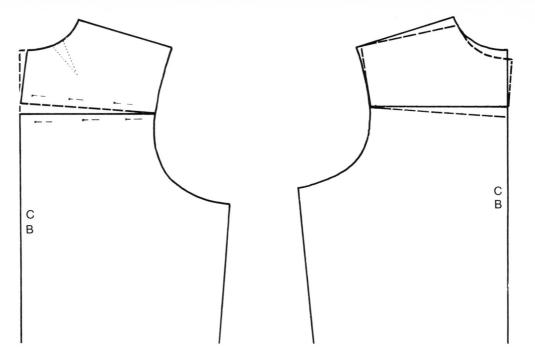

Figure 8   *Round shoulders*

Figure 9   *Erect back*

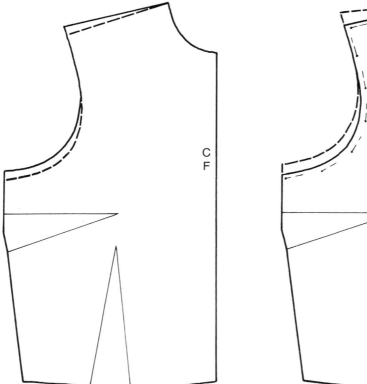

Figure 10   *Sloping shoulders*

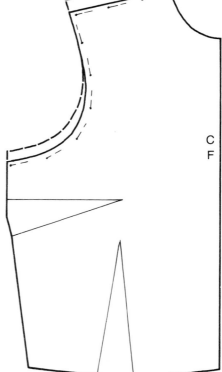

Figure 11   *Square shoulders*

back and front armholes. Lift the shoulder line at the armhole edge as illustrated in Figure 11. Add the amount required by pinning the pattern to paper and marking the new line. Raise the same amount at the underarm to retain the size and shape of the original armhole.

Narrow shoulders Make the alteration to the back and front patterns. Draw lines A–B–C from the middle of the shoulder line 10 cm down, then across to the armhole line (see Figure 12). Cut the pattern along this line from A to B to C. Overlap line A–B for the amount required to adjust the shoulder measurement. Draw new shoulder line.

Broad shoulders Make the alteration to the back and front patterns. Draw line A–B–C, 5 cm in from armhole edge, 10 cm down and across to armhole line (see Figure 13). Cut line A–B–C. Open up the pattern. Pin to paper. Draw new shoulder line.

Neck line too tight The garment pulls and forms wrinkles at the base of the neck. Mark new neck line, making it 1.3 cm lower at shoulder point to CF (see Figure 14). Lower the back neck line to match up with the front, taking off 1.3 cm at shoulder point, 1 cm at CB.

The same alteration must be made to the neck line facings.

Low bust Move the bust dart down to the new position (check that both sides of the dart are the same length). Shorten the waist dart. Adjust the bodice side seam line (see Figure 15).

High bust Move the bust dart up to the new position. Lengthen the waist dart (see Figure 16).

Large waist line Adjustments to the waist measurements are made by adding to the side seam and reducing the dart allowance. This will increase the waist measurement. Divide the amount needed

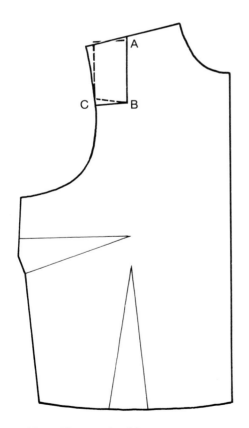

Figure 12   *Narrow shoulders*

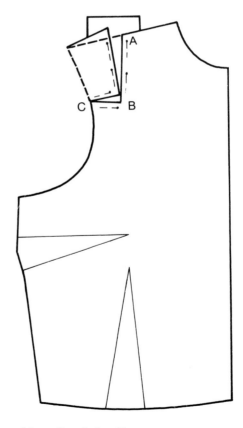

Figure 13   *Broad shoulders*

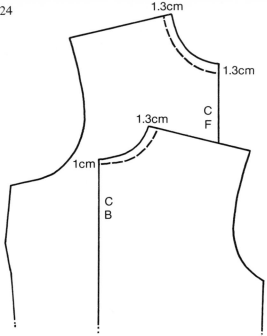

Figure 14   *Neck line too tight*

for the adjustment by the number of darts plus the seams (see Figure 17).

Small waist line Reduce the side seam and increase the dart allowance, dividing the amount needed for the adjustment by the number of darts plus the seams (see Figure 18).

Large abdomen The garment pulls out of shape above and below the waist line. The skirt rides up in the front if the garment is tight across the abdomen. Draw two lines through the bodice, A–B, C–D (see Figure 19). Cut along these lines. Open up the pattern for half the amount needed. Pin to paper. Mark new dart. Keep CF straight. Make the skirt adjustment in the same way.

Sway back Wrinkles appear at the CB waist line because of excess fabric in this area. The pattern needs to be shortened above and below the waist line to give a smooth fit. Cut the pattern at the waist line; fold out the required amount at the CB

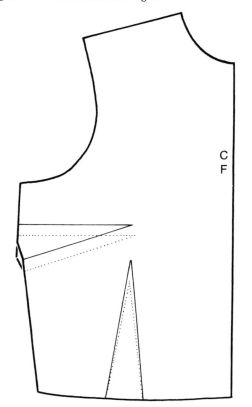

Figure 15   *Low bust*

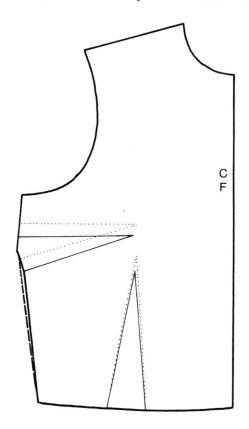

Figure 16   *High bust*

waist, tapering to nothing at the side seam (see Figure 20). Adjust the darts. The pattern cannot then be placed to a fold but must have a CB seam line. If this alteration is done to a pattern with a waist seam, it can be done in fitting by removing excess fabric from the bodice and skirt waist lines.

Sleeve alterations Alter above or below the elbow whenever the alteration is required (see

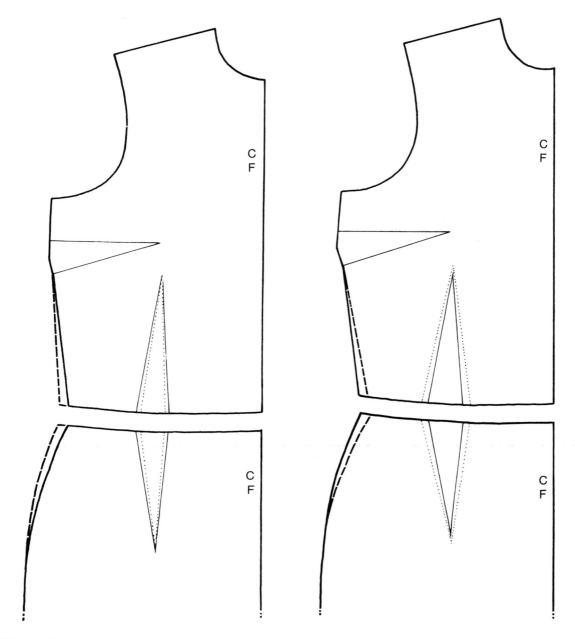

Figure 17   *Large waist line*   Figure 18   *Small waist line*

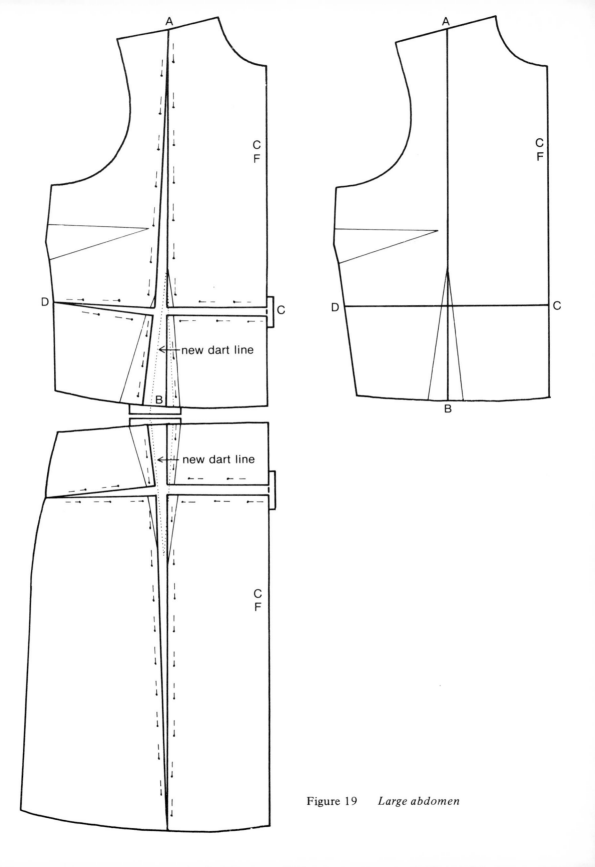

new dart line

new dart line

Figure 19   *Large abdomen*

Figure 21). Check that the elbow darts are kept at their correct position (see Chapter 2 on measuring the overarm – measurement number 9).

Large upper arm Increase the sleeve width but not the sleeve head measurement. Cut across at underarm, A–B (see Figure 22). Then cut through the pattern to the sleeve head, C–D. Spread the pattern at C. Pin to paper.

Skirt alterations Shorten the skirt pattern by trimming away the required amount from the hem line, measuring accurately at regular intervals (see Figure 23).

Lengthen the skirt pattern by adding the required amount at the hem line (see Figure 24). Pin to paper.

Large hips Add a quarter of the amount needed

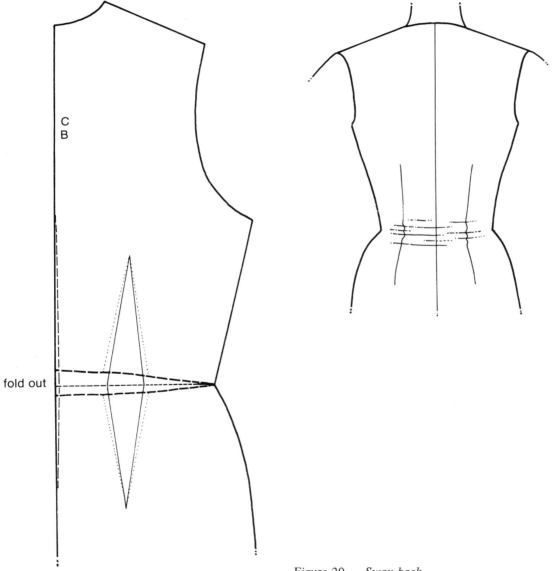

C
B

fold out

Figure 20   *Sway back*

to shorten

to lengthen

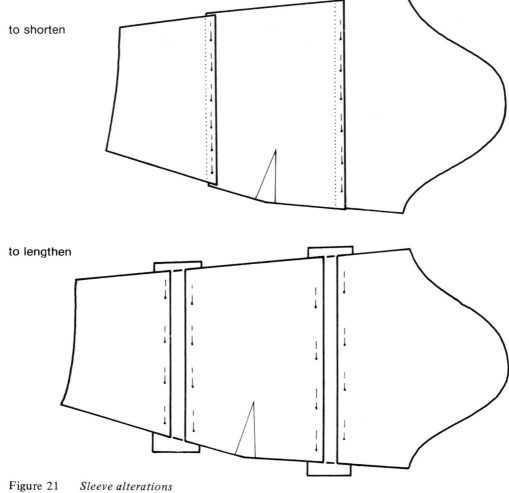

Figure 21   *Sleeve alterations*

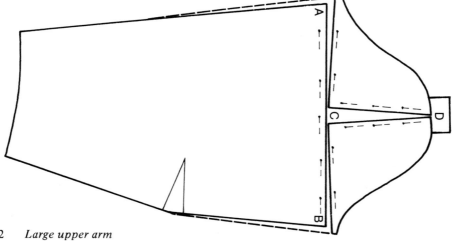

Figure 22   *Large upper arm*

on both front and back skirt patterns at the side seams, tapering from the waist to increase the measurement at hip line (see Figure 25).

Large derrière Cut the pattern through the dart to the hem line, A–B (see Figure 26). Cut across the pattern at the base of the dart from CB to side seam, C–D. Open up the pattern and pin to paper. Reduce to waist measurement by increasing the dart.

Trouser alterations Fold out the amount required to reduce the length either at point A, B or C (see Figure 27).

Cut through the pattern at point A, B or C (see Figure 28). Open up the required amount to increase the length. Pin to paper.

To give a longer length to the back crotch and more width across the back, draw a line from CB to

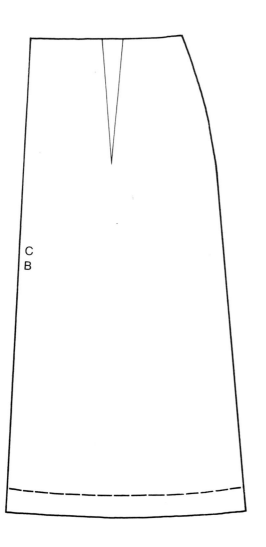

Figure 23   *To shorten pattern*

Figure 24   *To lengthen pattern*

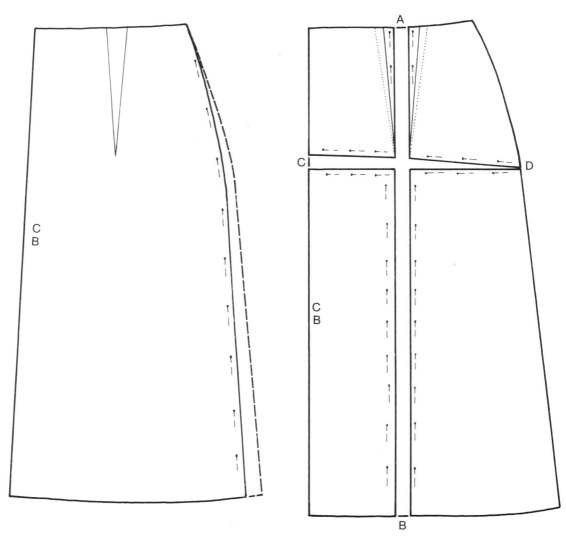

Figure 25   *Large hips*   Figure 26   *Large derrière*

the side seam 7–8 cm above the crotch line (see Figure 29). Open up the pattern the required amount at CB, tapering to nothing at the side seam. Pin to paper.

To avoid pull at the crotch line, give more width to the crotch at the top of the inside leg by increasing the pattern (see Figure 30). Adjust both front and back patterns if necessary. Check that the inside leg seam is central.

To avoid bagging and too much fullness at the crotch, reduce the width of the crotch and the top of the inside leg (see Figure 31). Adjust the front

and back patterns if necessary. Check that the inside leg seam is central.

To give extra length over a large abdomen area, cut the pattern from CF to the side seam 7–8 cm above the crotch line (see Figure 32). Open up the pattern at the CF tapering to nothing at the side seam. Pin to paper.

When all the adjustments have been made to the pattern, check the measurements of the pattern pieces against the body measurements, allowing for 'ease', which is included in all commercial pattern pieces.

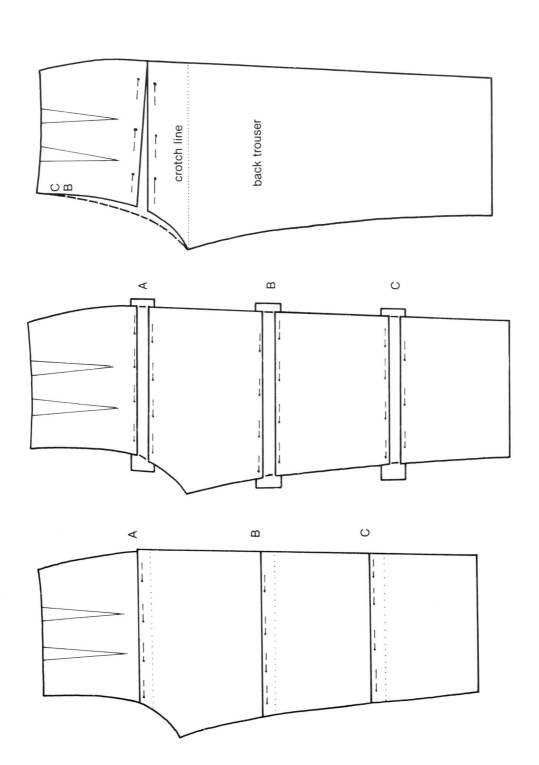

crotch line

back trouser

Figure 29

A

B

C

Figure 28 *To lengthen*

A

B

C

Figure 27 *To shorten*

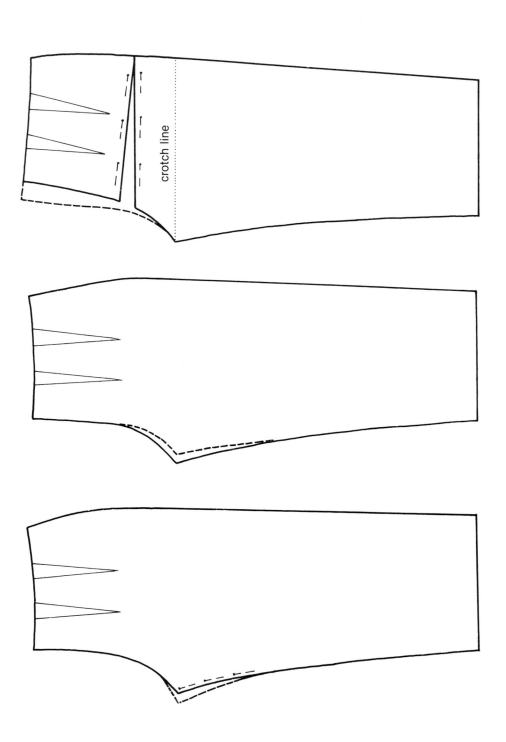

crotch line

Figure 32   *Large abdomen*

Figure 31   *To reduce crotch*

Figure 30   *To widen crotch*

Tools and equipment

After reading this chapter you will be able to:

1   Choose the correct tools and equipment for the work in hand.

2   Care for and store these correctly.

3   Use each piece of equipment to achieve a professional finish.

A dressmaker needs good tools and it is worth investing in good quality pieces of sewing equipment. Always buy the very best that you can afford – it is cheaper in the long run. The tools listed and discussed below are essential to work efficiently and to produce good results.

Cutting

Large table

A large, flat surface is essential to place the fabric on to for cutting out, so that it can be checked for grain, flaws and the matching of patterns. A cutting out board is now produced commercially which is a useful piece of equipment and well worth the money.

Cutting out shears

These scissors should be 18–20 cm long and should be made of a good quality steel. The blades must be long, smooth and sharp. One blade should be narrow and pointed, the other blade wider and rounded at the end. Try to avoid dropping scissors as this can lead to a distortion of the balance of the blades, which could make an uneven cut. It can also result in a little chip (almost invisible) out of the cutting edge, which would give a blunt spot on the blade, and this could snag the material when cutting out.

Remember – cutting out shears should only be used for cutting fabric and *never* be used for any other purpose. Left-handed shears are obtainable for those who work left handed.

Scissors

In addition to cutting out shears, it is advisable to have several pairs of scissors to use for different purposes.

a   *Scissors 12–14 cm long*, with pointed ends to the blades, are useful for clipping seam allowances.

b   *Buttonhole scissors* are designed to cut open buttonholes accurately. The blades are adjustable and can be set to cut the length required.

c   *Scissors 14–16 cm long* are useful for cutting paper and sewing thread. Both paper and sewing thread blunt the blades of scissors, and it is advisable to have this extra pair in your work box for this purpose.

d   *Electric scissors* are not essentially necessary for general sewing purposes, but they are a very useful tool for those who have difficulty in manipulating large shears for any period of time. People with arthritis in their hands find electric scissors very useful.

Measuring

To achieve a good fit to a garment, accurate measurements must be taken. The correct measuring tools are essential and must be used correctly. They should always be in good condition. Some pieces of equipment need replacing at regular intervals; otherwise the use of old and worn tools can easily cause inaccuracies. For example, the same tape measure should be used for measuring throughout the making of each garment to keep the measurements consistent.

Tape measure

Select a plastic or fibreglass one. Cheap tape measures become ragged at the edges and tear. Some types of tape measure stretch easily; therefore it is worth spending time and the extra money to purchase a good one. Metal tips on each end of the tape help to keep the edges from fraying. The numbers are printed clearly on both sides of the tape, and the tape is usually 150 cm long.

Metre stick

This is not an expensive piece of equipment. Available in wood, metal and perspex. This is a very useful tool for checking the grain of material, marking hems and for other general marking purposes.

Hem marker

A hem marker provides a quick and accurate method of measuring hem lines. They are available in various types: (a) pin it marker, and (b) chalk marker. Both types work in the same maner. The pin it marker is more accurate and leaves the pins firmly secured along the hem line. The chalk marker tends to leave thick chalk lines, and it is difficult to remove the chalk from certain fabrics.

Marking

There are various tools which can be used to mark pattern symbols, and each one has its uses. It must be remembered that some fabrics can only be marked in certain ways, while other fabrics can be marked easily, quickly and accurately by using other tools.

Tracing wheel

The tracing wheel may be needle pointed or blunted and is available in plastic or metal. The wheel rolls along the pattern lines, transferring the marks to the fabric through dressmaker's carbon paper, leaving a row of small dots as the guide line for construction.

Tailor tacker

A commercial tool is available for this purpose.

Tailor's chalk

Tailor's chalk is made in small, flat, 5 cm squares and comes in various colours. It should be used carefully as some of the chalk is not easily removed from the fabric.

Chalk pencil

This is easier to use than tailor's chalk and gives a thinner line to the pattern symbols and is, therefore, more accurate.

Tailor's wax

Used on wool fabrics, it must be used with caution as it is not easily removed. It is harder than tailor's chalk and is opaque.

Pins and needles

Pins

Dressmaker pins must be chosen carefully because the wrong type of pins can cause the fabric to mark if they are poorly finished. Buy dressmaker pins of fine steel and buy in boxes for storage purposes. Make sure that the pins are stored in a dry place to avoid rusting. Steel pins are more expensive but they are fine and sharp, which makes them much easier to use than coarse, blunt pins. The most useful length pin to use is 25 mm or 30 mm for general dressmaking use. Lace pins are available for very fine fabrics, and longer, coarse pins are useful for working with heavy fabrics.

Needles

In any craft the use of the correct needle for the work in hand is of utmost importance, and this is so in dressmaking. Attention must be paid to choosing the correct type and size of needle. A fine needle is required for fine fabrics and a coarse needle for heavy fabrics. Sewing needles are numbered. The smaller the number the coarser the needle. For general sewing purposes a no. 8 is an average size and suitable for medium-weight fabrics.

The following list is provided as a general guide for the choice of the correct needle and its use.

Sharps Used for most general sewing purposes, medium length, round eye.

Betweens A short needle, useful for working buttonholes. Known as a tailoring needle.

Crewel Used for embroidery and also useful for general sewing. Medium length, oval shaped eye which is larger than sharps and more easily threaded.

Darners A long, coarse needle with long, narrow eye.

Beading Very fine and long, especially designed for beadwork.

Straws Known as a millinery needle. Long, fine and very flexible.

Leather Specially designed with a three cornered point to work leather and suede. The sharp point pierces the skin easily without tearing the work.

These types of needles cover all the various uses for dressmaking. Machine needles are discussed in Chapter 5.

Thimble

The thimble is worn on the middle finger and should be used for all sewing. It must fit the middle finger comfortable and snugly, as it is used for pushing the needle through the work.

Threads

Sewing thread is constructed from various fibres, so care must be taken when selecting a sewing thread to work on a fabric. Always select the best one to suit the fabric, considering colour, weight, fabric content.

The following list is provided as a guide for the choice of threads:

Mercerized sewing cotton Most often used for general sewing. It is available in different thicknesses and in a wide range of colours. Use no. 50 for light-weight fabrics, no. 40 for medium to heavy-weight fabrics.

Sewing cotton Stronger than mercerized cotton. It has a dull appearance. Cotton thread does not always give good results in machine stitching.

Tacking cotton Used for tacking the garment together for construction and for fitting. It has a dull appearance with a hairy surface, which

enables the thread to remain in the garment pieces and does not easily fall out, as would mercerized thread, which has a smooth surface.

Sewing silk Made from pure silk fibres, it is strong and has good elasticity. It should always be used for silk fabrics, and because it has an animal fibre content it should be used for quality wool fabrics. It also gives good results on synthetic fabrics as it produces a very fine stitching line.

Synthetic sewing thread Available in various types and thicknesses with a range of colours. It is advisable to choose this type of thread when working with any fabric with a synthetic fibre content, because it has the correct amount of stretch and elasticity to work the fabric correctly.

Elastic thread Used for shirring, to be worked either by hand or machine. It is a fine, elastic thread which can be used to give a decorative finish on a garment.

Embroidery thread Made from cotton or silk, it is used for hand embroidery designs. Embroidery thread is also available in a fine strand suitable for machine work.

Buttonhole twist Used for decorative stitches and hand worked buttonholes. Made from silk it is sold on small spools. Buttonhole twist is also produced in synthetic yarn.

Having considered your fabric and the thread required, you should always test the thread on a scrap of fabric to ensure that you obtain the correct tension and stitch length required.

Never use a synthetic thread on a cotton or linen fabric as the thread requires a different tension from the fabric. Also iron temperatures are different for thread and fabric. For example, a cotton fabric will take a high temperature iron - a synthetic thread will melt under too hot an iron.

Consider next your choice of needle and balance this with the thread and fabric being worked. To help you find the correct balance follow the chart in Figure 33. Note the numbering of machine needles: the smaller the number, the finer the needle.

Dress stand

A dress stand is a useful addition to your sewing equipment, and it is a great aid in garment construction. It enables you to check the overall line

Fabric weight	*Fabric type*	*Thread*	*Sewing needles*	*Machine needle*	*Stitches per 2.5 cm seams*	*Decorative top stitching*
Sheer	Lawn, voile, chiffon, fine lace, organdie, georgette	Silk, mercerized cotton no. 50, synthetic	10–12	70	15–20	–
Light-weight	Gingham, satin, taffeta, muslin, crepe, jersey, dress cotton, woollens, tricot	Silk, mercerized cotton no. 50, synthetic	8–10	70–80	12–15	6–12
Medium	Denim, flannel jersey, crepe, needlecord, twill, dress linen, brocade, velvet, terry cloth	Silk, mercerized cotton nos. 40–50, synthetic	8	80–90	10–12	6–12
Heavy	Denim, tweeds, twill, gabardine, coatings, sail cloth	Silk, mercerized cotton nos. 36–40, synthetic	6–8	90–100	10	6–8
Stretch fabric	Polyester, nylon, jersey, tricot, cire	Mercerized cotton no. 50, synthetic	10	70 ball point	12–15	–
Bulk	Courtelle, acrilan, fake furs	Mercerized cotton nos. 36–40, synthetic	6–8	90–100	8–10	–

Figure 33

of a garment, but it is not intended to be used for fitting purposes.

Checking the style lines, collar and rever shapes, pocket placements, yoke lines and button positions is made easier and carried out more accurately by using a dress stand, and it is a great aid when attaching a lining to a garment. Never fit a garment on to a larger sized stand than the garment measurements, as this can cause strain on the seams and distortion in the finished garment.

You can test the different effects in the combination of fabrics of different colours and textures, checks and stripes by placing the fabric on to the stand before cutting out. The dress stand is also used for modelling purposes by dress designers when draping or creating a style in mull (muslin or lightweight calico), directly on to the stand, to be used later as a pattern.

chapter 5

Sewing machines

After reading this chapter you will be able to:

1 Recognize the different types of sewing machine.

2 Use a sewing machine.

Selecting a sewing machine

A sewing machine is a major piece of equipment and an expensive one, probably something one would buy only once or twice in a lifetime. It is essential therefore to consider the matter carefully before making a final decision to purchase.

Consider exactly what is required from the machine. How much is the machine going to be used? What sort of work is it going to be used for?

Visit a reputable sewing machine supplier and ask for demonstrations on various machines. Always try out the machine yourself as well as watching a demonstrator use it.

Consider cost. Is it necessary to buy a full automatic model with a range of embroidery stitches and other attachments? Consider space available for storage. Is it better to buy a portable model or to have the machine set into a cabinet?

Having decided upon the type of machine, check the following points before making the purchase:

Is the operation smooth and quiet with easy speed control?

Are directions clear and easy to read for threading bobbin and top thread?

Is it easy to adjust tension, pressure, stitch length?

Is the light so placed that it is focused directly on to the work?

Is there a good after-sales service?

What guarantee does the machine carry?

Servicing

Although a machine company may offer a good after-sales service, careful use and regular attention when the machine is in use will help to keep it in good running order and so give good service.

Read the instruction book carefully and follow the instructions; oil and clean regularly. Do not neglect oiling the machine. It is better to do this often, using the oil sparingly, than to leave it months before oiling and then using far too much oil. After oiling run the machine for a couple of minutes to distribute the oil. Before using check that no oil is spotting the machine. This could mark the fabric.

Some fabrics cause fluff to form under the feed dog. Check this and brush regularly to remove fluff and dust. Cover the machine after use.

Machining techniques

It is essential to understand the way the machine works and to be able to control the machine in order to sew successfully.

Use the machine to master controlling the stitching line by working samples of various types of stitching.

Use striped and checked fabric to practise straight stitching. The lines in the fabric and the edge of the presser foot will act as a good guide to keeping the stitching straight.

Practise controlling the machine by stitching curved lines, working slowly to manipulate the fabric to form a good curve.

Practise stitching corners by stitching in one direction, pivoting by raising the presser foot and turning the work while the needle is still down, then continue stitching in a different direction.

Secure the beginning and ending of seams by practising reverse stitch control. Good machining makes for a good finish to a garment, and it is worth mastering.

Types of machine

Straight stitch

Limited use but useful for stitching seams and neatening the edges of seams in dressmaking. Can be used for free embroidery. Certain attachments are available for this type of machine.

Semi-automatic

With a swing needle this type of machine has various uses: neatening seams, buttonholes, roll hemming, twin-needle sewing. Some semi-automatic models have a small number of decorative stitches built in.

Fully automatic

This type of machine has a wide variety of uses with a large number of combinations of built-in decorative stitches used for embroidery work.

It is impossible to give instructions to use a particular type of machine as they all differ, but there are basic rules applicable to all machines which are helpful.

Needle

Check that the needle is the correct size and type for fabric being worked. Insert the needle with the take-up lever at its highest point to avoid damaging the needle (see Figure 33 for needle sizes).

Make sure that the clamp screw is tight so that the needle will not drop out. Check and change the needle regularly. A blunt needle will miss stitches and may damage some fabrics.

Twin needle – check that the machine will take this needle.

Bobbin

Identical threads must be used for top and bobbin threading. The bobbin must be wound evenly. Check whether the bobbin is placed so that the thread travels in a clockwise or anti-clockwise direction according to instruction book.

Threading

Follow instructions set out for the machine. It is essential to practise threading, the setting of various dials and cams and the use of different attachments so that when stitching a garment or piece of work the process is successful.

Tension

If the tension of a machine is not correct, the seams may pull out or pucker.

Read instructions on adjusting tension. Check diagrams with stitching to arrive at a correct tension.

Attachments

The use of attachments in dressmaking varies in the type of work undertaken and the type of machine used, but there are certain attachments used regularly on all machines for general dressmaking purposes.

Piping foot

This is a one-pronged foot enabling the machine needle to be placed right up to the stitching line without obstruction. Used to apply zip fasteners and for stitching corded piped seams.

Blind hemmer

A foot attached to a machine to work an invisible hem finish. It is placed against a fold in the fabric picking up a thread in the fold and the under fabric alternately as it stitches the hem.

There are many other machine attachments available for different purposes to get full use out of the machine. It is worth spending time with the instruction book and the machine to learn all the different uses the machine has to offer.

chapter 6

Pressing

After reading this chapter you will be able to:

1 Recognize essential pieces of equipment.

2 Use the equipment correctly.

3 Achieve a professional finish knowing how, when and where to press.

Equipment

The following equipment listed is essential to good dressmaking; it is worth investing in these tools and learning to use them efficiently.

Iron

Must be thermostatically controlled. A steam iron is useful for pressing when a little moisture is required. The surface of the iron must be kept clean. Fusible interfacings can mark the iron and soil the surface; such marks are then transferred to the fabric.

Ironing board

The cover must be clean and washable and the board should be well padded.

Sleeve board

A small version of the ironing board. Useful for pressing small areas such as short seams.

Tailor's ham

A firm, oval shaped cushion used for pressing over curved surfaces for moulding and shaping. Available in a number of sizes.

Padded roller

A long, cylindrical roller used to prevent an imprint forming on the right side when a seam is being pressed. This can easily be made from a broom handle 60 cm long, padded evenly with sheet plastic foam and then covered with a clean cotton cover.

Tailor's clapper

A wooden shaped block useful when steam pressing woollen or difficult to press fabrics. By beating the clapper on to the seam, it traps the steam for a longer time to give a firmer, flatter finish to the seam.

Pressing cloths

Used to prevent shine on the RS of the fabric. The cloth must be clean and free from seams or hems as these can cause ridges to appear on the fabric. Linen cloth is useful for general pressing. Muslin is useful for light-weight fabrics. Use damp when moisture is needed.

Needle board

A narrow board made up of a bed of upright wires. The wire side of the board preserves the character of the fabric being pressed. Used for pressing pile and nap fabrics, for example, velvet. The boards are available in a number of sizes. Store in a dry place to prevent rust forming on the bed of wires.

Pressing techniques

Always test a sample of the fabric to determine moisture, temperature and pressure.

Moisture

Most fabrics need some moisture for pressing. Use a damp cloth for this purpose, but never use a wet cloth as too much moisture will mark the fabric and will also give an over pressed look. Do not move the garment from the pressing board while it is still damp, as handling can stretch the fabric. Allow to dry before proceeding with the next stage. The use of a dry pressing cloth will help to remove moisture and 'set' the seam.

Temperature

Check the thermostat setting on the iron and test on a sample of fabric. An iron that is too hot will cause certain fabrics to shine, mark and even burn.

Pressure

Never allow the full weight of the iron to rest on to the fabric. Control the lifting and lowering movement of the iron to keep an even pressure on the fabric.

Pressing during construction of a garment

Press on as small an area of the garment as possible, for example, darts before edges are crossed with a corresponding seam. Overall care during pressing will eliminate unnecessary problems.

Remove all tackings and pins before pressing to avoid marking the fabric with stitch or pin imprints. Do not fold up the garment pieces after pressing as this will cause further creasing. Lay flat.

Seams

Never join sections of a garment without first pressing the seams of both. For a smooth seam, press over the machine stitching, then press the seam open. This will give a flat finish. To emphasize a style line, press both edges of the seam to the same side. To avoid seam imprints on the right side of the fabric, press over a padded roller.

Curved seams should be moulded over a tailor's ham to press in the curve of the style line to maintain the 'rounded' look. Armhole seams are lightly pressed towards the sleeve. Press waist seams towards the bodice.

Darts

Place the dart area over the curve of the tailor's ham and press along the stitching line, then to one side.

Do not press beyond the point of the dart. Waist line darts and shoulder darts are pressed towards the centre; bust darts and elbow darts are pressed downwards.

Double pointed darts are clipped in the centre at the widest point so that they can be pressed flat.

When heavy-weight fabrics are being worked, all darts need to be cut through the centre and pressed open. This avoids bulk and a ridge forming on the right side of the fabric.

Dart tucks are not pressed beyond the stitching line.

Gathers and shirring

There should be no creases in a gathered section. Do not move the iron from side to side, but move it into the gathers towards the stitching line. When a plain section joins a gathered one, be careful not to press beyond the seam line from the plain side.

Pleats

Tack before pressing. Press along the fold line and the stitching line on the wrong side. Remove the tacking stitches, then press on the RS using a dry cloth to prevent shine.

Zip fasteners

Press on the WS up to, but not over, the metal teeth and fastener. Press on the RS over a padded surface. These precautions must be taken to avoid imprints on the fabric. Check the temperature of the iron when pressing a nylon zip setting as an iron that is too hot will cause the nylon to melt.

Hems

Press upwards from the lower edge. Do not press around the skirt hem as this will stretch the hem line. Do not press the full depth of the hem as this will cause a ridge along the hem line. When pressing on the right side, press over a well-padded surface to prevent an imprint forming.

Neck lines

Press over a sleeve board or tailor's ham. Avoid stretching the neck line by holding the curved line carefully. Press from the outer edge of the collar towards the neck line.

Final pressing

If correct pressing techniques and procedure have been carried out during the construction of a garment, very little final pressing is required. Move the garment with care to avoid creasing. Never over press.

To remove shine or press marks

1   Place the garment right side up over the ironing board; hold a steam iron above the marked area. While the fabric is damp from the moisture, brush with a piece of the same fabric or a stiff brush.
2   Place a piece of napped wool cloth, then a damp cloth, over the marked area. Steam by holding a hot, dry iron close to the pressing cloth but not on it. When the nap has been raised, place a dry cloth over the area; hold the iron close to it so that the heat dries the fabric.

Different methods of pressing are used on different fabrics. The following list is provided to give guidance to some of the different treatments required.

Cotton and linen 'Hot' iron setting. Press on the wrong side using moisture. Then press dry.
Wool 'Moderately hot' iron setting. Use a damp cloth. To avoid imprints, do not put too much pressure on to the fabric.
Silk 'Moderately hot' iron setting. Press dry or over a light-weight, damp pressing cloth. Take care to avoid spot marks from too much moisture.
Rayon 'Low heat' iron setting. Press on the wrong side using very little moisture.
Synthetic 'Low heat' iron setting. Press on the wrong side using a damp pressing cloth. Avoid forming creases in the fabric as these are difficult to remove once they are pressed in.
Blended and mixture fabrics Check on the fibre content and use a setting required for the lowest temperature.
Pile fabrics Steam over a velvet board or over a padded surface. Press as little as possible. Deep pile fabrics often require finger pressing only.
Metallic Use a 'cool' iron setting. Press as little as possible. It is essential to test a piece of fabric for correct treatment.
Lace/embossed Press both of these fabrics over a padded surface on the wrong side only to avoid damaging the surface design.
Laminated Use a temperature suitable for the top fabric. Do not press directly on to the sheet foam. Use a dry pressing cloth.

chapter 7

Fabric lay, cutting, marking

After reading this chapter you will be able to:

1 Understand the structure and designs of a fabric in relation to 'lay-out' in preparation for cutting.

2 Cut out all garments accurately.

3 Transfer the pattern symbols to the fabric.

Preparation of the fabric

It is essential to check the fabric carefully before laying on the pattern pieces. Open up the fabric and check for flaws in the weaving, printing or dyeing. If the fabric is flawed, mark it with a coloured thread so that it can be avoided when the pattern pieces are laid on. Each pattern piece is labelled and numbered. Check that all the pattern pieces are available to cut the complete garment.

Check that fabric is on correct grain to avoid distortion of the style lines of the garment; otherwise it will not 'hang' correctly on the figure. Check the 'grain' on woven fabrics by pulling a crosswise thread at the end of the fabric and by pulling the fabric into shape at each end.

Press out any creases and refold fabric if necessary.

Plain, coloured, woven fabrics present no problem, and the pattern pieces can be dovetailed and placed facing both directions (see Figure 34).

Some fabrics have 'one-way' designs such as floral patterns, geometric shapes and irregular checks (see Figure 35).

Such fabrics must be treated as 'with nap' for lay-out purposes, placing all the pattern pieces in the same direction. Checks, stripes or any other patterns in the fabric must be matched at seam lines on corresponding pattern pieces. This is done by matching balance marks (notches) when laying out

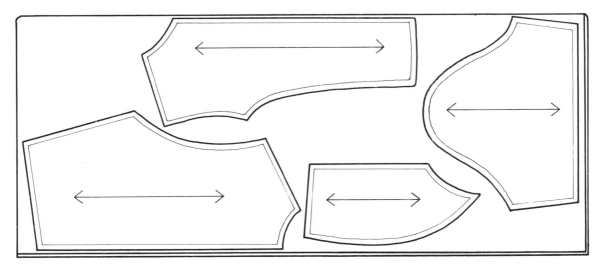

Figure 34   *Lay – without nap showing dovetailing of pattern pieces*

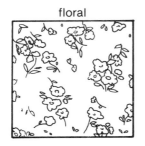
floral

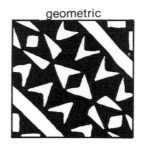
geometric

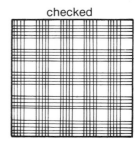
checked

Figure 35

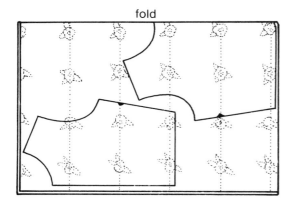
fold

Figure 36

Figure 37

and when pinning the pattern pieces into position. It is essential to do this in order to match up the patterns in the fabric design during the construction of the garment (see Figures 36 and 37).

Certain other fabrics also require 'one-way' lay, because the surface pile on the fabric runs in one direction; examples of these fabrics are needlecord, corduroy, velvet, face cloth, camel hair, satin and fur fabrics.

Preparation of lay

Plan the complete lay by placing the main pattern pieces on the fabric as economically as possible. Other smaller pieces are then laid on to the fabric. Check 'lay' carefully for 'straight of grain'; this must be done by measuring with a tape measure or ruler accurately at both ends of the grain line symbol. It must lie parallel to the selvage edge of the fabric.

Cutting

Hold the scissors so that the long pointed blade is underneath and the rounded blade on top of the fabric. Take long, firm cuts using the full length of the blades; do no snip or use short cuts as this will give a jagged edge to the cutting line. Keep the material flat. This gives accuracy to the cutting line. Cut around the notches carefully. Never cut the notches out of the seam allowance as this will weaken the seam (see Figure 38).

When cutting out on single fabric, reverse the pattern for the second piece, for example, sleeves (see Figure 39).

When all the pieces are cut out, each symbol must be transferred to the fabric.

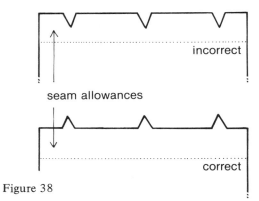

seam allowances

Figure 38

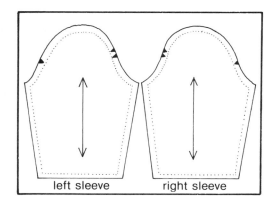

Figure 39   *Pattern reversed for cutting on single fabric*

Methods of marking

Thread marking

Trace tacking Turn back the edge of the pattern so that the seam lines lie on the fold of the pattern. Mark the seam lines with tacking stitches. This is a useful method when working on difficult to handle fabrics as it gives a clear indication of the fitting lines (see Figure 40).

Tailor tacking A reliable and effective way to transfer pattern symbols. The stitch forms a loop which is cut through the centre between the two layers of fabric, leaving small stitches on both sides of each garment piece (see Figure 41). Do not make the loop more than 4 mm as a stitch that is too large easily pulls out.

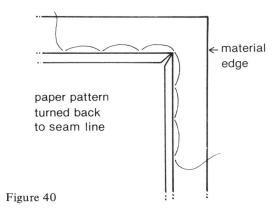

Figure 40

Tracing wheel

Used with dressmaker carbon, this is a quick, easy method of transferring pattern symbols. This tool must be used carefully on the wrong side as the fabric can easily be marked or snagged.

Tailor's chalk

Use on the wrong side of the fabric. A quick way to transfer pattern symbols, but has the disadvantages of rubbing off and of only marking one side of the fabric.

Leave the pattern pieces on the fabric until all the symbols have been marked. The pattern pieces can then be lifted off and the garment tacked together for fitting.

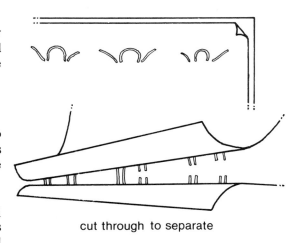

cut through to separate

Figure 41

chapter 8

Fitting

After reading this chapter you will be able to:

1 'See' the correct silhouette for the garment.

2 Achieve the correct line and 'hang' for the style.

3 Assess accurate positioning of style detail.

Fitting is an important part of dressmaking. Skill in fitting comes with practice in observing every detail of the garment. This is only achieved by building up experience in a variety of situations concerned with the fitting of garments in different fabrics and for different figure types.

Fabric must be considered so that it can be best used in relation to texture, drapability and the placing of focal points of the fabric design to form an attractive feature of the garment being made. A garment must fit correctly to be comfortable to wear and also to look attractive. It must fall gracefully over the figure and never pull out of shape.

Careful measuring of the figure (see Chapter 2) and accurate alterations to the pattern (see Chapter 3) should eliminate any major fitting problems. The garment must be tacked together on the correct seam lines for the first fitting, including one sleeve. Shoulder pads should be available to give the garment the necessary padding and the correct 'hang' from the shoulders.

The garment must be worn right side out when it is being tried on, and an underslip must be worn for dress and skirt fittings as this enables the garment to hang smoothly over the figure. Foundation garments, if normally worn, must be used for fitting purposes; otherwise the correct line of the garment will not be achieved. It is also important to wear the correct shoes as varying heel heights can affect the figure posture and alter the appearance of the overall silhouette.

The following points should be helpful as a final check during fitting:

1 The garment should conform to the figure contours according to the design.

2 The amount of 'ease' must be considered; this varies with the style of the garment, the fabric being worked and current fashion trends.

3 The garment is supported by the shoulders and the figure contours; the shoulder seams should fit smoothly, extending from the base of the neck to the shoulder bone.

4 All vertical seams located at CF, CB and SS should not incline in any direction but sit absolutely vertical.

5 Seaming incorporated into the design of a garment should sit smoothly with no strain or twisting.

6 Darts should sit smoothly and point to the fullest part of the body curve, ending about 2.5 cm below the fullest part.

7 Neck lines should sit correctly on the body and should not gape or pull.

8 Collars are a focal point of design and should sit properly on the figure without becoming distorted, whether the body is moving or remaining still.

9 Armholes should fit smoothly around the arm; a sleeveless dress should not gape at the underarm point.

10 Sleeves should hang comfortably and give room for movement. The grain line should run from the shoulder seam to the little finger.

11 Openings should give sufficient room to enable the garment to be put on and taken off, without straining any part of the garment.

12 Fastenings should be marked and tacked into position so that the opening can be closed properly during fitting. No fastening should pull apart or gape.

13   Design details, such as godets, pleats, gathers and tucks, should fall smoothly on the figure.

14   Pockets, tabs and other decorative detail must be positioned correctly and must lie flat so that they do not detract from the smooth line of the garment.

15   Hem lines must be level and a uniform distance from the floor along the entire length of the skirt circumference.

Trouser fitting

16   Trousers should fit smoothly over the curves of the body and should not strain or bag.

17   The waist should be comfortably snug.

18   The hip width and crotch depth should give sufficient room to sit comfortably.

19   The thigh area should not pull.

20   The crotch area should not pull or crease.

21   Outside leg seams should fall straight to the floor.

22   Inside leg seams should not pull or incline sideways.

23   Hems should fall freely and should not crease by falling on to the instep.

chapter 9

Modelling

After reading this chapter you will be able to:

1   Recognize requirements for modelling.

2   Understand direction of 'grain'.

3   Develop a 'seeing eye' with regard to proportion and line.

Modelling is a method of making a pattern by using the art of manipulating the pattern muslin to create a style on a dress stand. To the dressmaker with creative ability, this method of producing a pattern can be very satisfying.

To model successfully, the dressmaker must have a good practical knowledge of dressmaking, fully understand the grain of material, have a sense of proportion and line and a keen sense of accuracy.

Most cutting out is done on double material; therefore it is only necessary to model on the RS of the stand, unless the style is draped or has an asymmetrical line, or the figure has irregular measurments. The stand should then be padded accordingly.

Tools, equipment and materials

Dress stand
Mull – muslin or light-weight calico
Pencil
Pins
Scissors
Tape measure
Sketch of design

Use the right weight material for the work. It must be soft and easy to manipulate. If the mull is semi-transparent, the dress fabric can be seen through it when cutting out.

General rules of modelling

Keep the grain of the pattern muslin true. The selvage grain runs from neck line to hem (see Figure 43, A–B) and from sleevehead to wrist (see Figure 43, C–D). Unless the style requires otherwise, the weft thread lies horizontally across the figure (see Figure 43, E–F).

Study the grain of the mull when modelling as this is the grain line to follow when cutting out the garment fabric. Do not model any part of the garment on incorrect grain.

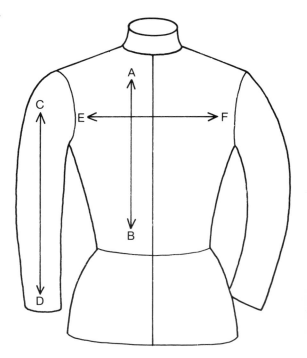

Figure 43   *Direction of grain lines*

Figure 42   *Draped styles*

Use the selvage if it has a good clean edge; otherwise fold over on the grain and press a crease line. A straight edge must give a true line to begin modelling.

Use a clean, straight edge to define CF and CB lines of bodice and skirt.

Modelling a basic bodice pattern

Front

Pin selvage to CF of stand allowing 4 cm above the shoulder point. Place the pins horizontally as illustrated in Figure 44. Keep the weft grain straight across the figure, and pin at armhole level. Pin dart at waist taking out 4 cm, tapering to nothing at bust point.

Pin dart at underarm to bust point (approximately 10 cm long). Mark neck line with a clear pencil line. Clip in several places to allow the mull to sit correctly along the neck line (see Figure 45).

Cut the neck line pointing the scissors around the neck, using the rounded blade of the scissors towards the stand. Leave a 2 cm seam allowance.

Pin mull to fit waist line pinching the material between the thumb and forefinger 1.3 cm to add ease on to the pattern.

Cut away surplus mull to 4 cm below waist and 5 cm beyond underarm line, up to the shoulder line area.

Back

Pin selvage to CB of stand allowing 4 cm above shoulder line. Pin as directed for front bodice. Pin dart at waist 7.5 cm from CB. The base of the dart should be no more than 4 cm and should be 10-12 cm long, tapering off to nothing at the tip of the dart.

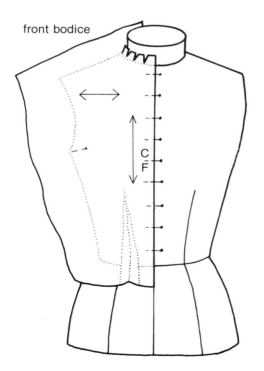

front bodice

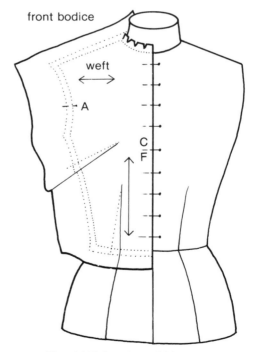

front bodice

weft

Pin at 'A' denotes width across chest

Figure 44   Figure 45

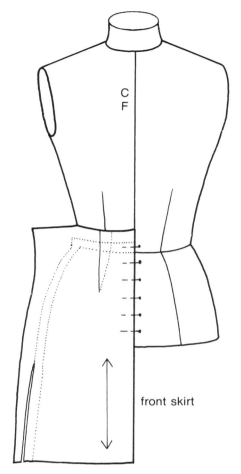
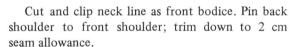

Figure 46

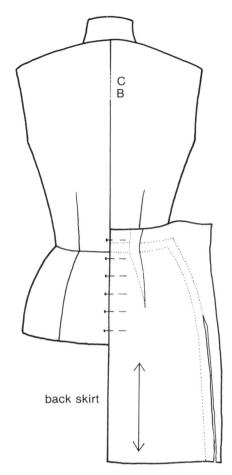

Figure 47

Cut and clip neck line as front bodice. Pin back shoulder to front shoulder; trim down to 2 cm seam allowance.

Cut away surplus material 4 cm below waist and 5 cm beyond underarm line.

To complete bodice pattern

Mark underarm seam line. Pin front bodice to back bodice; trim seam allowance to 2 cm.

Complete marking at front and back waist, trim seam allowance to 2 cm.

Armhole

Measure width across chest; mark with pin at A (see Figure 45). Measure width across back, and mark with pin. Mark curved armhole line from these pins keeping the line high and rounded at the underarm to avoid cutting a 'V' shape, which would not give an accurate fitting line. Trim to within 2 cm of armhole.

Remove the pattern from the stand; mark seam lines and darts with coloured thread. Mark CF, CB, grain line and balance points.

Basic skirt pattern

Front

Pin selvage to CF of stand, placing the pins horizontally as illustrated in Figure 46. Allow 4 cm above the waist line. Keep weft grain straight across the figure at hip level. Line up waist dart with front bodice. Pin dart at waist, tapering to nothing. Smooth material to side seam allowing for ease; trim away surplus material to 5 cm.

Back

Work as for front skirt pattern (see Figure 47). *Dart length* Front skirt - 10-12 cm; back skirt - 12-15 cm.

To complete skirt pattern

Mark waist and side seams accurately. Trim away surplus material to a 2 cm seam allowance. Remove from stand. Mark seam lines and darts with coloured thread. Mark CF, CB, grain line and balance points.

Tack bodice and skirt patterns together. Return to dress stand to check dart positions, line and straight of grain for accuracy.

chapter 10

Focus on stitches and seams

After reading this chapter you will be able to:

1   Select and work suitable stitches used in dress-making processes.

2   Recognize seams and their uses in construction techniques and decorative detail.

It is essential to use the correct thread for the fabric being worked. A slightly darker shade thread than the fabric will work in better than a lighter colour. See Chapter 4 for selection of threads.

Stitches

Hand sewing is an important part of dressmaking, and the right stitch in the right place is essential. The principles of good hand-sewing techniques are:
1   Work on a smooth flat surface.
2   Use correct thread and size needle.
3   Begin and end firmly securing the stitching line with two or three back stitches.

Tacking stitches (Figure 48)

Even tacking   The stitches must be the same length, 5 mm long; this is used for tacking seams together for fitting.

Diagonal tacking   Used for holding interfacings in place. Take a long, vertical, slanting stitch and a short, horizontal stitch to form a diagonal stitch.

Uneven tacking   Used to mark centre lines for fitting. Make a long stitch on the RS and a short stitch on the WS.

Slip tacking   Used for matching up stripes and surface patterns. Work on RS of fabric. Fold fabric along fitting line. Place to corresponding seam line. Tack folded edge, taking the needle through the fold and picking up a stitch directly opposite this point, on the underside.

Ease

Ease in seams must be evenly distributed and held by pinning at right-angles when tacking together.

These are temporary stitches and will be removed during construction of the garment (see Figure 48).

Hand stitching on garments is used mostly for hem finishes, edge neatening, hand-stitched zip setting and decorative details.

All hand stitching must begin and end with firm, secure stitches. Take two or three small backstitches, and when working on a folded edge, run two or three small stitches through the fold. The tension must be even or the work will pucker and give an amateur finish.

Running stitch

Used for hand gathering, this is the most basic stitch used in hand sewing. The stitches are even in length and no more than 3 mm long. Take two or three stitches on the needle and weave the needle in and out of the fabric (see Figure 49).

Backstitch

Worked close together, the stitch is as firm as machine stitching. Work on the RS, taking one small stitch at a time. The stitch must come back to the end of the previous stitch, and there should be no spaces between the stitches (see Figure 49).

Stab stitch

Used at each end of a pocket opening. The stitches are worked using a stabbing movement through the fabric making a very small stitch on the RS and a longer stitch on the underside (see Figure 49).

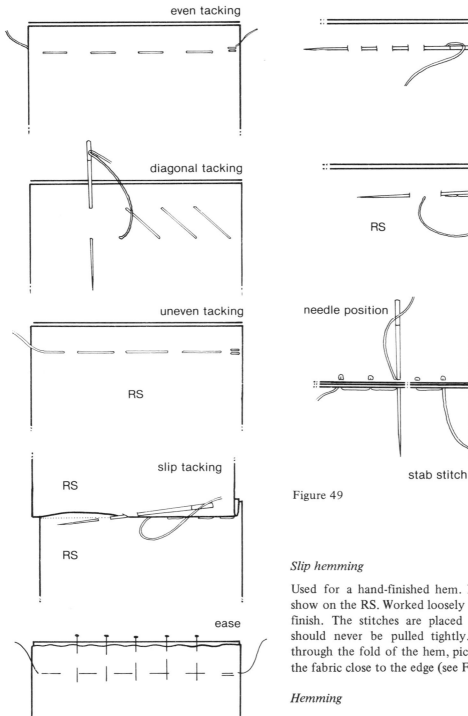

Figure 48   *Tacking stitches*

Figure 49

Slip hemming

Used for a hand-finished hem. No stitches should show on the RS. Worked loosely for almost invisible finish. The stitches are placed 1.3 cm apart and should never be pulled tightly. Bring the needle through the fold of the hem, picking up a thread of the fabric close to the edge (see Figure 50).

Hemming

Used to hold folded edges in place (for example, a lined yoke) and for narrow hems. The stitches should be small and even in space and direction (see Figure 50).

Whipping

A stitch used on light-weight and sheer fabrics to neaten a raw edge with a rolled hem. The edge is rolled tightly in a forward movement between the left thumb and forefinger (see Figure 50).

Loop stitch

Used on a decorative finish, for example, lace appliqué, or as a neatening stitch. Hold the work upright, working the stitches close together; loop the thread under the needle to form the stitch (see Figure 51).

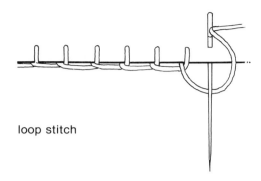

loop stitch

buttonhole stitch

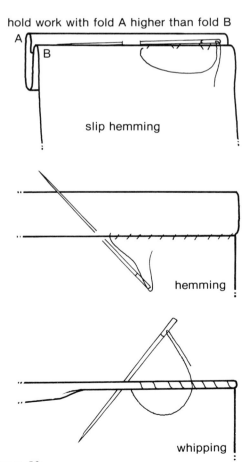

hold work with fold A higher than fold B

slip hemming

hemming

whipping

Figure 50

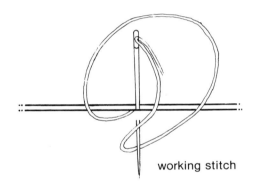

working stitch

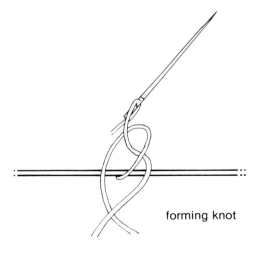

forming knot

Figure 51

Buttonhole stitch

Used on hand-worked buttonholes, it is an upright
stitch. The thread is twisted from left to right under
the needle, forming a knot at the cut edge of the
buttonhole. The stitches must be equal in length
and closely spaced for strength. Draw thread upwards to form knot (see Figure 51).

Seams

It is essential to choose the correct seam for the garment type and use and for the fabric used. Seams
must be neatened or enclosed during construction.
Every seam must be accurately stitched to finish on
the fitting line.

   Curved seams require clipping at regular intervals,
approximately every 1.5–2 cm, to enable the seam
to lie flat.

   Eased seams must be machine stitched on the
eased side to check that the ease is being distributed
evenly.

   Seams must be stitched with the correct machine
tension; otherwise they will pucker and pull tightly,
or will be too loose and pull out.

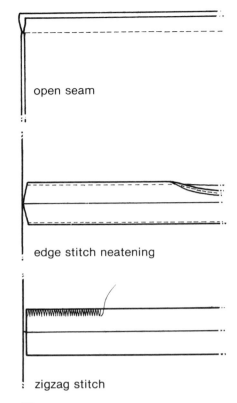

Figure 52

Open seam

Machine stitch along fitting line. Press open or to
one side (see Figure 52).

Neatening

a   *Edge stitch*   Turn under and crease at each
      edge of seam allowance. Machine stitch along
      the edge of creased line. Used on light-weight
      fabrics (see Figure 52).
b   *Zigzag stitch*   Set machine to zigzag stitch and
      reinforce the edge of the seam allowance. Used
      on light to medium-weight fabrics (see Figure
      52).
c   Overlock   Worked on an overlocking machine
      or a machine with the overlocking stitch. Gives
      a firm finish to seam allowance edges. Used on
      all fabric weights.

French seam

Used on light-weight fabrics for lingerie and children's wear. It is a double seam used to enclose raw

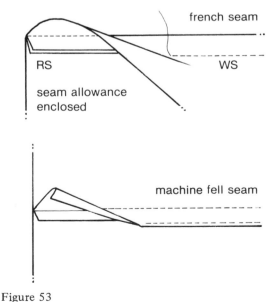

Figure 53

edges. Place WSS together; machine stitch 2 mm outside the fitting line. Trim close to stitching line. Press. Turn to WS. Machine stitch on fitting line, enclosing raw edges (see Figure 53).

Machine fell

A strong seam used on shirts, blouses and pyjamas. Work as for open seam with WSS together. Press open. Trim down one edge of seam allowance to 3 mm. Turn under 5 mm on remaining edge. Press. Top stitch folded edge over trimmed edge (see Figure 53).

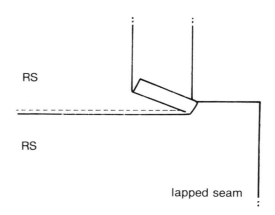

Decorative seams

Lapped seam
Press edge of fitting line to WS. Lap folded edge over remaining edge, keeping the seam allowances even on WS. Top stitch on RS in same colour or contrast colour thread.

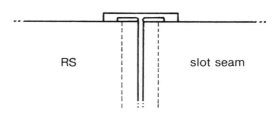

Slot seam
Work as for open seam, tacking together along fitting line. Press open. Cut strip of fabric 6 cm wide × length of seam. Mark fitting line on centre of strip. Place this mark to the garment fitting line. Tack backing strip to garment. Machine stitch 5 mm each side of fitting line. Remove tacking. Press. Neaten.

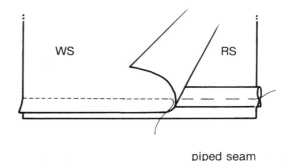

Piped seam
Cut crosswise strip 2 cm wide × length of seam. Place RSS together; fold strip in half lengthwise. Tack strip, placing folded edge 2mm beyond fitting line. Place corresponding piece to first piece. Machine stitch. Press to one side.

A piping cord may be enclosed inside the strip to give a corded effect. The cord must be pre-shrunk.

Strap seam
Work as for open seam WSS together. Trim seam allowance to 5 mm. Press open. Cut strip 3 cm wide × length of seam. Press 5 mm to WS, each side of strip. Place WS strip to RS garment, centring strip over seam line. Top stitch close to edges of strip. See Figure 54 for an illustration of these four decorative seams.

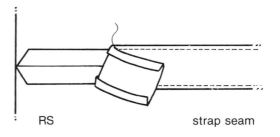

Figure 54   *Decorative seams*

Techniques and Processes

Part One dealt with choosing suitable fabrics and styles, with the tools and equipment required to work efficiently. It also dealt with what to use, how and when to use it, so that the preparation work is done successfully.

Part Two deals with various processes used in constructing the garment. Experience is gained from trying different methods and working with different fabrics and styles.

Begin by choosing a simple style in an easy to handle fabric and produce a good result. Then, by being more creative and adventurous, additional processes may be tackled successfully. It is wise to extend into more difficult processes *or* more difficult fabrics rather than both together.

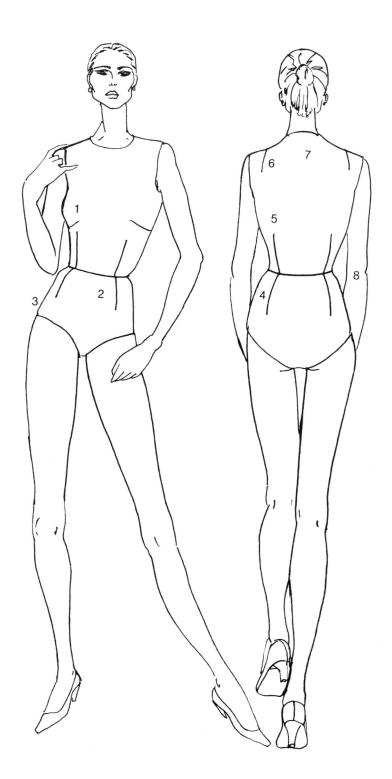

Figure 55

chapter 11

Shaping to fit – controlling fullness

In this chapter you will be given:

1   Ideas for creating 'style lines' to accommodate the curves of the body.

2   Instructions for using the various methods for shaping a garment.

In garment construction the work is three dimensional. The fabric is cut to the pattern shapes and joined together to make up the garment.

There are certain body curves which must be considered when designing and constructing garments. The numbers below correspond to the numbers shown in Figure 55.

Front

1   bust
2   abdomen
3   hip curve

Back

4   back hip
5   lower shoulder blades
6   upper shoulder blades
7   round shoulders (dowager's hump)
8   elbow

Shaping is formed by use of:

1   curved seams
2   darts
3   tucks
4   pleats
5   gathers

Curved seams

A style line falling over the curve of the figure is shaped with the forming of a curved seam. The seam must run down or across the fullest part of the figure to give balance to the style of the garment. For some uses of curved seams in design, see Figure 56.

Figure 56   *Curved seams*

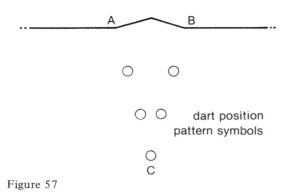

Figure 57

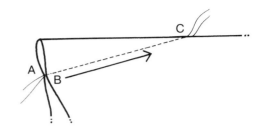

Figure 58

Darts

Darts are wedge-shaped areas, which are shaped to the body by holding the fabric in a rounded shape and so removing excess width or length of the fabric. The fabric is stitched to take in the amount needed to give the garment a close fit over the body curve (see Figure 57, AB–C).

Darts must be tacked in position before fitting – never machine stitched – because adjustments sometimes need to be made depending upon the figure being fitted.

Bust darts should point to the fullest part of the bust and end approximately 2.5–3.5 cm below.

Hip darts should end just above the fullest part of the hip; their approximate length should be 10 cm for the front skirt and 12.5 cm for the back skirt.

Elbow darts should point towards the tip of the elbow; their approximate length should be 7.5 cm.

Shoulder darts should point towards the shoulder blades; their approximate length should be 7.5 cm.

Back neck darts should point towards the shoulder blades; their approximate length should be 7.5 cm.

Making a dart

Pin, tack and machine stitch the two edges of the dart through the seam lines, working from the wide end to the point, taking care to taper the dart off to nothing, as illustrated in Figure 58. If the stitching ends abruptly at the point of the dart, it will be impossible to get a smooth line on the RS of the garment.

The ends of the threads must be secured. These can be darned back into the fold of the dart, or strengthened by reverse stitch when machine stitching the dart. This reverse stitch must be accurate and follow the original line of stitching. Remove tacking.

Pressing darts

Darts should always be pressed over a curved surface to keep the proper curve to accommodate the body contour.

Neck darts
Shoulder darts } are pressed towards the CF or CB
Waist line darts

Bust darts } are pressed downwards
Elbow darts

Each dart is pressed on the WS. Press along each side of the stitching line, in the direction of the stitching (from wide end to point). Then press the dart to one side.

For a double pointed dart, clip at the widest point of the dart to release the fabric. This will enable the dart shape to lie flat and form a smooth contour. Press the dart from end to end along stitching line. Then press the dart to one side.

When working with thick fabrics cut through the centre of the dart and press open. This will reduce bulk (see Figure 59). For designs using darts, see Figure 60.

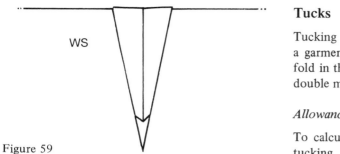

WS

Figure 59

Tucks

Tucking can be used both as a decorative feature of a garment and to hold the fullness in place. It is a fold in the material secured by stitching through the double material on the RS of the garment.

Allowance of material

To calculate the amount of material necessary for tucking, allow three times the finished width of

Figure 60   *Designs showing use of darts*

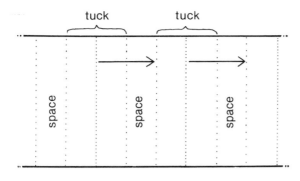

Figure 61

each tuck, for example, 1 cm tuck requires 3 cm fabric (see Figure 61).

Tucks can vary in width: vertical tucks from pin tucks to 1.5 cm, and horizontal tucks from 1.5 cm to 4 cm. They can be evenly spaced or arranged in groups. The space between the tucks should not be less than the finished width of the tuck, running vertically, horizontally or diagonally, depending upon the effect required and the style of the garment.

Types of tucks

Pin tucking

A very narrow tuck making a fine ridge and so giving very little fullness. Pin tucks are only two or three threads wide. Used on fine fabrics, for example, lawn, chiffon.

Group tucking

Worked together in groups of three or more tucks. Used on front and back bodices, blouses, dresses, children's wear.

Cross tucking

Tucking worked in two directions to give a very effective design. Work the cross tucking before laying the pattern piece on to the fabric. Press all the tucks in one direction before making the cross row.

Shell tucking

Used as a decoration on lingerie. Tack and press the tucks before shell stitching. Work fine running stitches for 0.5 cm, then take two stitches over the tuck. Draw the thread tightly before continuing the running stitches. These can be worked by hand or by machine (use special attachment).

Released tucks

The fabric is stitched to form a short tuck and then it is released to give a soft, folded effect. Worked on the RS or the WS. The tucks are evenly spaced. The ends of the stitching must be kept in a straight line.

Twin needle pin tucking

Worked on machines that will take a twin needle (see Chapter 5). This type of tucking can be worked with cord to give a raised tuck. A shadow tuck effect can be achieved on a fine fabric by using a coloured cord which will show through the tuck.

Diagonal tucking

Successful diagonal tucking needs practice and skill in working with fabric on the cross grain, as the tucks are machine stitched and pressed on the true cross. Careful handling is necessary to prevent stretching and distortion.

Tucking can be worked by hand or by machine. Stitching must be accurate and even. Work the stitching so that when fastening off, the thread comes to the underside of the tuck when the tuck is pressed.

Machine thread must always be a perfect colour match for a good finish, unless contrasting colour is used to give a decorative finish.

Tucks are always pressed flat. Vertical tucks are normally pressed away from the centre front of the garment unless the design requires directional pressing for a particular effect. Horizontal tucks are normally pressed downwards. For designs showing the use of tucks, see Figure 62.

Pleats

Pleats are used to give fullness and shape to a garment. Whether they are machine stitched and pressed flat over the hip line or fall unpressed from

Figure 62   *Designs showing use of tucks*

Figure 63   *Designs showing use of pleats*

the waist, they provide the extra width in a skirt to give ease in movement. For designs showing the use of pleats, see Figure 63.

Preparation for making pleats must be accurate. Work on a flat surface, carefully pinning the pleats and following the balance marks along the crease line. Check the width to make sure that the pleat is absolutely even by measuring carefully with your tape measure. Tack the pleat in position.

Allowance of material

The total amount of fabric used in pleating is three times the width of the pleat, for example, a 5 cm knife pleat requires 15 cm of fabric (see Figure 64).

Pressed pleats

Pressed pleats have the crease line pressed in position the entire length of the skirt. This gives the garment a crisp, tailored look. The free edges of pressed pleats can be machine stitched to keep the knife edge in place. This must be done after the hem has been finished.

Pleats are stitched on the right side or wrong side of the garment depending upon the finish required.

Right side stitching of pleats

Machine stitch for the length required, close to the folded edge of the pleat or 1 cm in from the edge (see Figure 65). The stitching at the turning point may be pointed or square.

Wrong side stitching of pleats

Machine stitch on the fitting line of the pleat on the WS for the length required. Finish off securely. Arrange the fold line to lie flat underneath the stitching (see Figure 66).

Pleats set over seams

Cut out the pattern pieces so that the seam is set under the pleat.

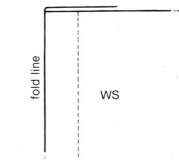

Figure 66

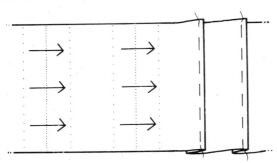

Figure 64

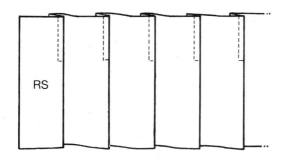

Figure 65

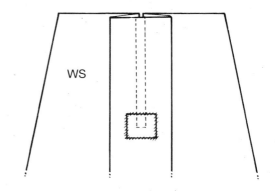

Figure 67

Strengthening the ends of pleats

Stay
Use a 4 cm square of canvas or firm material. Tack it to the WS at the point where the stitching will end (see Figure 67).

Tailor's bar tack
Using the machine thread, work four strands 0.3 cm long over the edge of the pleat on the RS. The threads must be close together; whip over the threads forming the bar. The bar tack must be worked very finely. This gives an inconspicuous result, and is mostly used on fine or light-weight fabrics (see Figure 68).

Arrow-head tack
Conspicuous and decorative. Use buttonhole twist of same colour as fabric. Work on the RS of the garment (see Figure 69).

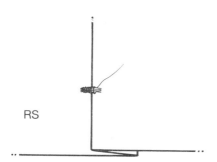

Figure 68

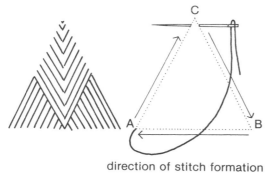

direction of stitch formation

Figure 69

Figure 70

Unpressed pleats

Unpressed pleats do not have the crease line pressed in place and are used to create a soft, graceful effect (see Figure 70).

Pleats with underlay

This type of pleat can be pressed or unpressed. The underlay is cut separately and machine stitched to the skirt side sections. The fitting lines are then brought together to form the pleat (see Figure 71).

Commercial pleating

Ready prepared fabric is available giving very narrow pleats made on the straight of grain and running lengthwise. This is known as accordian pleating and gives an attractive 'swing' to a skirt line. The amount of fabric needed for the pleating must be calculated by the commercial pleater.

Fitting alterations to pleats

Remove the tacking stitches at the upper edge of the crease lines. Take in or let out the amount required by tapering the pleats to the waist line. Any adjustment must be made to the underside of the pleat, keeping the spaces between the pleats uniform. Re-tack and press new pleat line.

Fabric choice for pleating

It is wise to choose a fabric with partial or whole natural fibre content to get the best results with pleated garments. Some synthetic fabrics cannot be pleated without special pressing equipment. Therefore fabric used for commercial garments for pleated styles are not always successfully pleated using the domestic iron. Wool worsted, wool mixtures and blends lend themselves to pleating.

Gathers

This is an easy and decorative way of controlling fullness on fine and light-weight fabrics. Gathers are used on bodices with shoulder or waist yokes, on sleeves with full sleeve-heads, on sleeves set into cuffs, on full skirts set on to a waist band or on skirts with a hip yoke as a feature of the design.

Gathering stitches are done by hand or by machine. Two rows of stitching will set the gathers better than a single row (see Figure 72).

Hand stitches must be the size of the finished gathers, approximately 0.3 cm long.

For machine gathering, use a long stitch – approximately 8 stitches to 2.5 cm. Work the gathering stitches within the seam allowance, placing the rows about 0.5 cm apart.

Avoid working over seams as this will make the gathering bulky and makes it difficult to adjust the gathers evenly.

Leave the ends of the threads hanging loosely so that the material can be drawn up to the required amount. When the required tension has been decided, secure the threads by winding around a

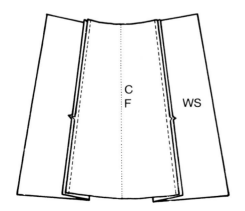

Figure 71

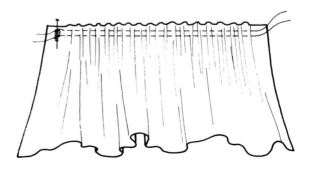

Figure 72

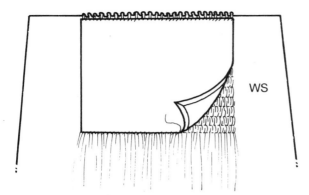

Figure 73

Figure 74   *Designs showing use of gathers*

pin, so that any further adjustments to the tension can be made.

When the tension has been checked for fitting on to the corresponding piece, the gathers can be secured firmly with a double backstitch on the wrong side of the garment.

Several rows of gathering can be used to give a more decorative finish to a garment. This is known as 'shirring' or 'gauging'. The rows of gathers must be evenly spaced. A cardboard guide will help to keep the rows even. Shirring is worked by hand or by machine. The same rule for stitch length applies to shirring as to gathering. Hand stitches must be the size of the finished gathers, approximately 0.3 cm. Machine stitches must be approximately 8 stitches to 2.5 cm.

Work hand shirring carefully, making sure that the stitches are placed directly underneath each other.

Where extra strength is required to support the shirring, a small piece of fine material should be cut to the shape of the shirring when drawn up. Turn under all the cut edges to neaten, or use a zigzag neatening stitch, and hem this piece of material to the shirring section on the WS of the garment. This is known as a 'stay' and will keep the shirring in place (see Figure 73).

Suitable materials for use as the 'stay' are net, muslin, fine silk or rayon lining. If a firm finish is required use a piece of organdie as the 'stay'. For some uses of gathers in design, see Figure 74.

chapter 12

Openings and closures

After reading this chapter you will be able to:

1 Select the correct opening for the style of the garment.

2 Select the correct fastening

3 Make the fastening for each opening.

Openings are necessary to pass the garment over the figure. They should be long enough to allow the garment to be put on comfortably without straining any seams. They should be easily accessible; the usual positions for openings are:

Centre front
Centre back
Side seam
Shoulder
Sleeve

Figure 75 is a guide to the correct position and length for openings.

For a blouse or dress with a short opening, the length of opening is:
CF   14–16 cm
CB   15 cm

A fitted dress will also require a side opening giving sufficient room to allow the garment to be put on comfortably.

Bodice openings

Separate facing

Transfer symbols from pattern to fabric. Attach interfacing to bodice fronts.

Place RS facing to RS bodice. Tack and machine stitch along seam line at neck edge and CF. Grade seam. Clip seam at neck edge. Neaten outer edge of facing (see Figure 76).

Press seams open. Turn facing to WS making sure that the seam line sits exactly on the edge of the opening. Make buttonholes (see Figure 77).

Grown-on facing

Transfer symbols from pattern to fabric. Attach interfacing to bodice front (see Figure 78).

Turn back facing along fold line RSS together. Tack and machine stitch along neck edge. Clip seam allowance. Neaten outer edge of facing (see Figure 79).

Type of garment	Centre front	Centre back	Side seam	Shoulder seam	Sleeve 7 cm from under-arm seam
Blouse			From 3 cm below under-arm to hem	10–12 cm	7–8 cm
Dress	56–60 cm	50–54 cm	26–30 cm	10–12 cm	7–8 cm
Flared skirt	20–22 cm	20–22 cm	20–22 cm		
Straight skirt	22–24 cm	22–24 cm	22–24 cm		

Figure 75   *Position of openings*

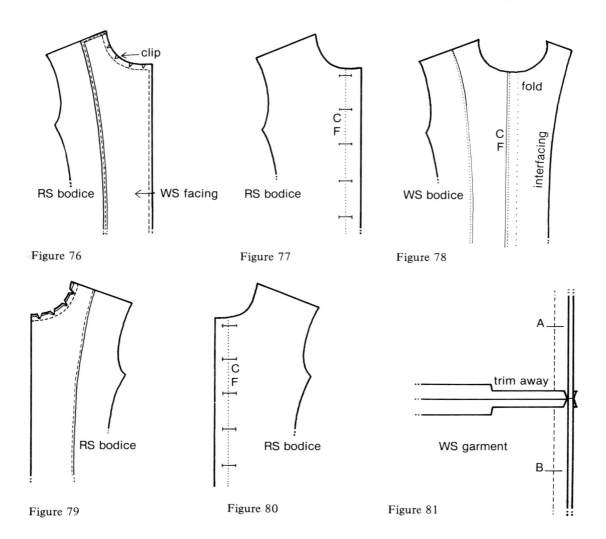

Figure 76

Figure 77

Figure 78

Figure 79

Figure 80

Figure 81

Press seam open, turn facing to WS. Press fold line and neck edge. Tack down to hold in place. Make buttonholes (see Figure 80).

Side seam opening (dress placket)

Side seam A–B = size of placket (see Figure 81). Trim seam allowance to 1 cm to avoid bulk at waist line.

Underlap

Turn seam allowance to WS 3 mm from fitting line. Tack and press this fold flat, extending 1.5 cm each end of opening point A–B.

Overlap

Working on dress front, turn back seam allowance to WS. Tack, press. Tack a further line 5 mm from turn back edge and across each end (see Figure 82).

The side seam placket is used with a concealed zip setting.

Sleeve openings

Faced opening

Cut a strip of fabric 7 cm × length of slash line + 3 cm. Neaten two long sides and one short side. Tack centre of strip over opening line. Machine

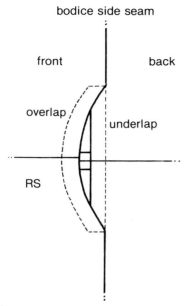

bodice side seam

front   back

overlap   underlap

RS

Figure 82

stitch 4 mm each side of centre line tapering to nothing at top of opening, taking one stitch across the top. Slash to point of stitching line (see Figure 83). Turn strip to WS. Press (see Figure 84).

Continuous strip opening

Cut strip of fabric on straight grain – twice length of opening × twice finished width of strip + 5 mm turnings.

Mark opening 7.5 cm from underarm seam. Slash this line (see Figure 85).

Pin, tack and machine stitch RS strip to RS opening. Take 5 mm seam allowance at sleeve edge; taper towards point of opening, raising needle to turn work carefully to avoid puckering the work (see Figure 86).

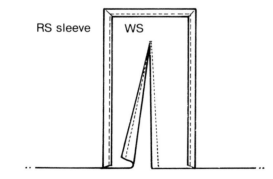

RS sleeve   WS

Figure 83

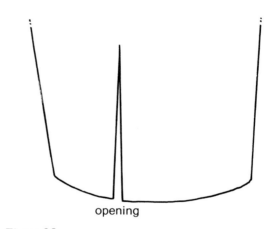

opening

Figure 85

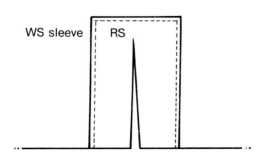

WS sleeve   RS

Figure 84

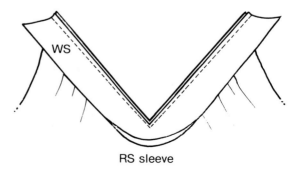

WS

RS sleeve

Figure 86

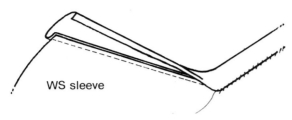

Figure 87

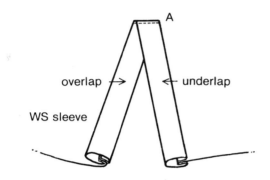

Figure 88

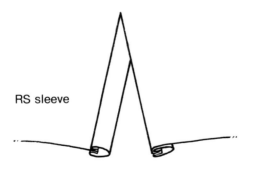

Figure 89

Turn in free edge of strip. Fold over, hem the folded edge to the stitching line. Do not allow the stitches to show on the RS (see Figure 87).

Press, fold strip underneath on RS of opening. The underlap must sit flat. Strengthen across top of strip – A (see Figures 88 and 89).

Fastenings

Fastenings are intended to close an opening which has been made to allow freedom to put the garment on and to take it off. With constant wear, openings are subjected to strain and should be strengthened where necessary. The fastenings must be finished off securely so that the opening stays closed and does not become distorted when it is fastened.

The following points must be considered when choosing and arranging the way in which an opening is to close.

1   The fastening must not restrict the opening in any way.
2   The type of fastening chosen must be suitable for the purpose.
3   The fastening must be suitable for the fabric to which it is being applied.
4   Garments to be laundered frequently require fastenings that will stand up to regular washing. Some plastic fasteners do not retain their colour and will not stand a hot iron.
5   Fastenings should be evenly spaced, and placed so that they do not pucker the garment or allow the opening to 'gape' when it is closed.
6   Fastenings are placed on double fabric to give them sufficient support. If it is necessary to place a fastening on single fabric, strengthen the fabric on the WS with a small piece of tape.

Types of fastenings

Hooks and eyes/bars

Attached by oversewing or buttonhole stitch (see Chapter 10). Buttonhole stitch gives a firm, strong finish to the edge of the fastening.

Hold hook in place with several stitches at top of hook. Work buttonhole stitch around base of hook. Insert needle outside hook and up through centre, pulling the thread to form knots around the hook (see Figure 90).

Figure 90

Press studs

Attached by oversewing or loop stitch. Attach ball side of stud to overlap. Attach socket side of stud to underside. Do not allow stitches to show on RS. The stud must be accurately placed to snap together firmly.

Socket is attached as illustrated in Figure 91.

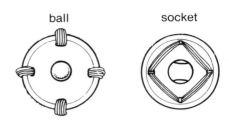

Figure 91

Rouleau loops

Cut crosswise strip 2.5 cm wide. Fold in half lengthwise RSS together. Machine stitch 5 mm from fold. Leave ends open. Using tapestry needle and thread, pull tube through to RS (see Figure 92).

Cut rouleau into short lengths for loops. Mark placement for loops. Complete fastening as in sleeve edge finish (see Chapter 15).

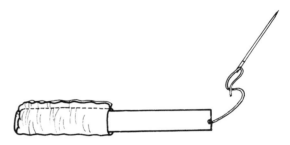

Figure 92

Thread loops

Made with buttonhole twist. Measure size of loop to fit button. Work four foundation stitches at edge of opening. Work loop stitch over the four strands. Place stitches close together (see Figure 93).

Lacing

Mark position of eyelets accurately. Outline small circle with running stitches. Pierce the fabric with stiletto. Work edge of circle with loop stitch using buttonhole twist (see Figure 94).

Metal eyelets are available for this purpose; they are attached to the garment by using a small tool supplied with the eyelets.

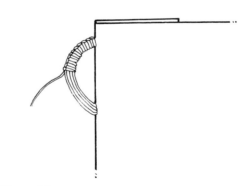

Figure 93

Self-fastening tape

Commercially produced in 2.5 cm wide strips available in a range of colours. The fastening is made in two separate strips that grip together. One side is covered with small hooks; the other side has a soft looped surface. Directions are given on the pack for stitching; this is a time saving fastening with a wide variety of uses.

Buttonholes

The length of the buttonhole depends on the diameter and thickness of the button. Allow 1–2 cm extra length depending upon the thickness of the

Figure 94

button. This is necessary to allow the button to pass through the buttonhole easily.

Mark the buttonhole on single fabric. Place a small piece of fusible interfacing behind the placement to give support to the binding. Cut a strip of fabric 5 cm wide and 2.5 cm longer than the buttonhole.

Cut a strip on the cross-grain to give maximum stretch when pulling the bind through to WS. With RSS together, tack the strip in position marking buttonhole line (see Figure 95).

Machine stitch 3 mm each side of centre and at each end of mark. Begin stitching at point A (see Figure 96); pivot at each corner by raising the presser foot to turn. Use a short stitch to give strong finish.

Cut buttonhole through all thicknesses clipping into corners. Pull strip through to WS (see Figure 97).

Make a small inverted pleat at each end of the back of the buttonhole. Press. Place small tacks to hold pleats in place (see Figure 98).

To complete the buttonhole, tack edges of binding on RS with diagonal stitches. Working on facing, cut from centre of the buttonhole to each end, clipping into corners (see Figure 99).

Turn in raw edges of facing. Hem, remove tacks. Press (see Figure 100).

Hand-worked buttonhole

Horizontal – one square and one round end.
Vertical – either two round or two square ends.

Worked on RS when the garment is completed. Mark buttonhole. Using a short stitch setting, machine stitch 2 mm each side of mark and across each end. Cut between stitching lines.

Commencing at square end, work buttonhole stitch (see Chapter 10), keeping the stitches exactly on the edge and even in depth (see Figure 101).

Finish square end by placing two or three strands of thread across the end. Work buttonhole stitch across the strands to give extra strength to the buttonhole (see Figure 102).

Machine-worked buttonhole

Most modern machines have attachments for working a buttonhole (see Chapter 5).

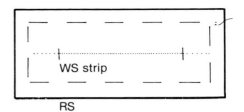

Figure 95

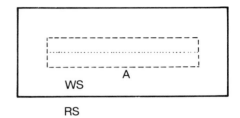

Figure 96

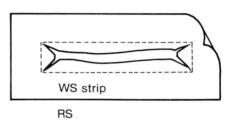

Figure 97

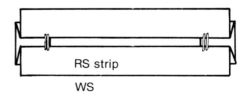

Figure 98

Buttons

Careful choice of buttons is important to the 'finish' of a garment. Buttons are sewn on to double fabric. Bring needle through the button to the RS, then back into the fabric. Place a pin over the

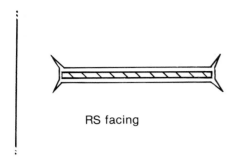

RS facing

Figure 99

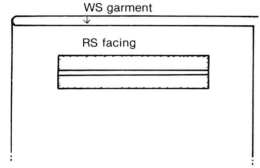

WS garment

RS facing

Figure 100

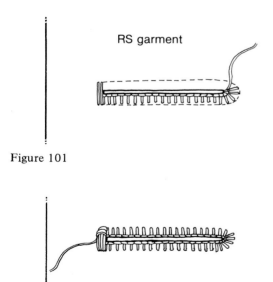

RS garment

Figure 101

Figure 102

button. Sew over the pin to form a thread shank at the back of the button, this prevents the fabric pulling. Wind thread around the threads under the button to form the shank. Finish off securely.

Zip fasteners

There is a wide variety of zip fasteners from which to choose; light-weight to heavy-weight, nylon and metal, skirt weight, trouser zips which are curved, open-ended and invisible. Choose the correct zip for the work in hand and the fabric being worked. Guidance is given on the packet.

A good range of colours is available. It is important to choose a good colour match. Measure the length of the opening to obtain the correct length zip fastener.

Concealed setting – overlapped

Apply the zipper before the neck facings are attached. Machine stitch CB seam to opening point. Press seam open. Clip into seam allowance at base of opening to within 2 mm of seam line (see Figure 103).

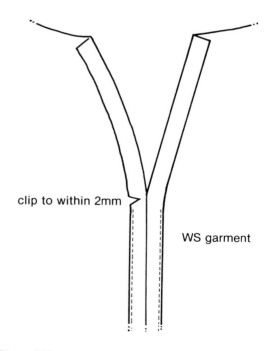

clip to within 2mm

WS garment

Figure 103

Press seam allowance from clipped edge to neck point, forming the underlap (see Figure 104).

Working on RS place zipper into opening with underlap placed to edge of teeth. Tack in position. Fold overlap to fitting line. Pin and tack zipper into place. Using piping foot (see Chapter 5), machine stitch underlap side, A–B. Machine stitch overlap, C–D–E (see Figure 105).

Semi-concealed setting – centred
Machine stitch CB seam to opening point. Press seam open. Do not attach neck facing. Tack opening to neck edge (see Figure 106).

Working on WS of garment, place zipper RS down to centre of tacked seam. Pin and tack 5 mm each side of centre line and across base. Machine stitch following the tacked line (see Figure 107). Remove tacking. Press.

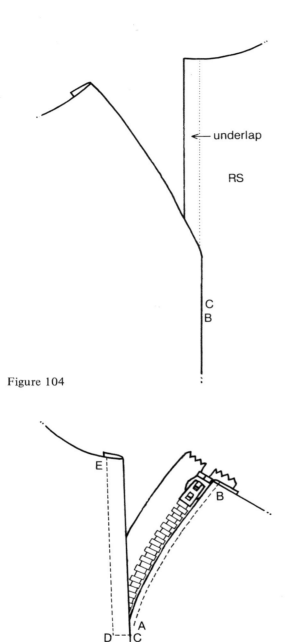

Figure 104

Figure 105

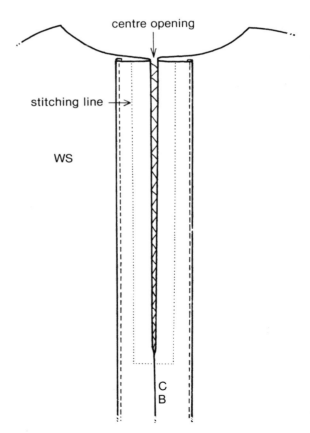

Figure 106

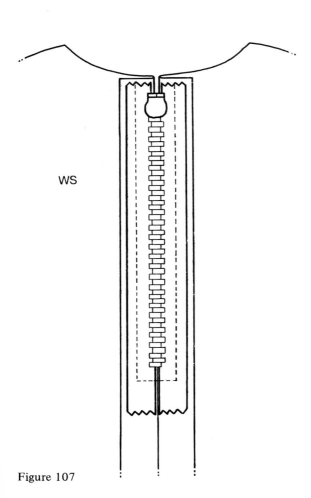

WS

Figure 107

chapter 13

Facings, bindings and edge finishes

After reading this chapter you will be able to:

1 Finish the raw edges of a garment by facings.

2 Finish the raw edges of a garment by bindings.

When finishing an edge of a garment with a facing or binding, the work must be finished to give a flat, smooth line without being stretched too tightly or allowed to crease along a curved line.

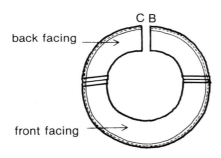

Figure 108

Neck facings

Round neck

Stay stitch to prevent stretching. Cut facing pieces, apply interfacing. Join front and back neck facings together at shoulders. Neaten outer edge of facing (see Figure 108).

Place neck edge of facing to neck edge of garment RSS together. Tack and machine stitch along the fitting line at neck edge. Clip turnings at 1.5 cm intervals, clipping right to the stitching line. This will allow the facing to lie flat when turned to the wrong side of the garment (see Figure 109).

Press, turn facing to wrong side (see Figure 110).

Secure facings at shoulder seams with several small stitches. Secure at CB by slip stitching the

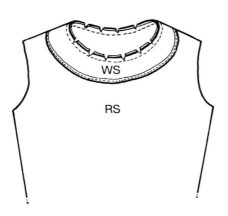

Figure 109

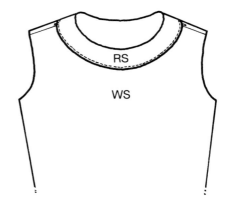

Figure 110

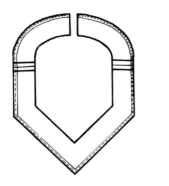

Figure 111

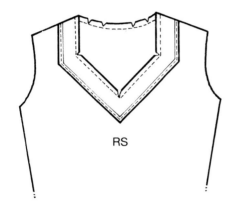

RS

Figure 112

WS

Figure 113

facing to the zipper tape. Never stitch through to the right side.

Shaped facing at neck edge

Machine stitch back facing to front facing at shoulders. Press seams open. Neaten outer edge of facing (see Figure 111).

Tack and machine stitch facing to neck edge. Clip into corners and into back neck curve (see Figure 112).

Press, turn facing to wrong side. Secure at shoulder seams (see Figure 113).

Right side finish

Place RS facing to WS garment. Tack and machine stitch at neck edge; clip turnings. Press. Turn facing to RS. Roll the seam line between the thumb and forefinger and tack through the double material close to the neck line. Turn under seam allowance at outer edge of facing, keeping the facing an even width. Tack. Finish with top stitching on RS of garment (see Figure 114).

Decorative finishes may be used, for example:
1 machine embroidery stitches
2 contrast colour thread
3 contrast colour facing

Scalloped edge facing

Place RS facing to RS garment. Tack and machine stitch facing into position, pivoting the needle at the points of each scallop. Notch at inner points and at 1.5 cm intervals along the curve of each scallop (see Figure 115).

Press over a small 'ham'. Turn facing to WS. Neaten outer edge of facing. Press, taking care to keep the shape of the scallops constant (see Figure 116).

Armhole facings

Join front facing to back facing. Press. Neaten outer edge of facing (see Figure 117).

Tack and machine stitch facing to armhole edge RSS together, matching seams at shoulder and underarm. Clip seam allowances. Press (see Figure 118).

Figure 114   *Use of right side facings to give decorative effect*

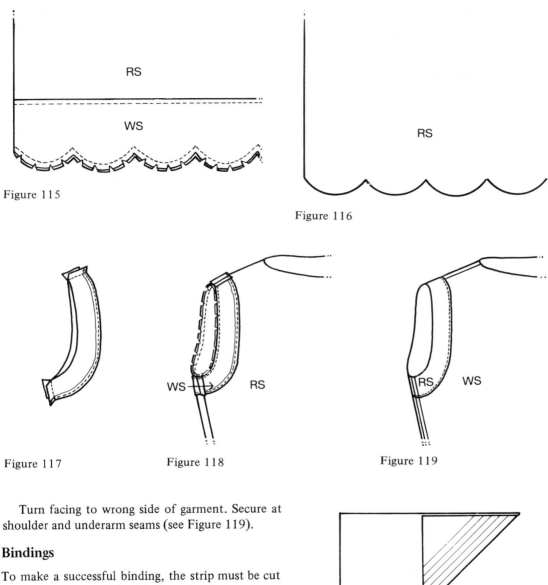

Figure 115

Figure 116

Figure 117

Figure 118

Figure 119

Turn facing to wrong side of garment. Secure at shoulder and underarm seams (see Figure 119).

Bindings

To make a successful binding, the strip must be cut on the true cross of the fabric to give the maximum amount of stretch.

Cutting crosswise strips

Fold the fabric over at right angles so that the warp and weft threads are parallel to each other. Press a crease along the fold line. From this crease, measure accurately (using a ruler) for the required number of strips. Cut the fabric along the marked lines (see Figure 120).

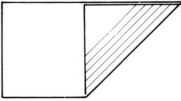

Figure 120

Joining crosswise strips

Place the RS of strips together on the straight of grain. If several strips have to be joined together, the joins must be in the same direction. Join the strips by placing them at right angles to each other (see Figure 121).

Press open. Cut off the extending triangles level with the edge of the strip (see Figure 122).

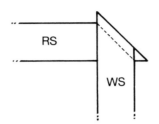

Figure 121

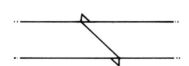

Figure 122

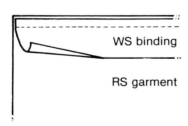

Figure 123

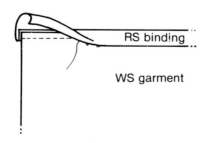

Figure 124

Application of crosswise strips

Binding straight edges

Cut strips twice the required width + 1 cm turnings. Join strips together for length required. Place RS binding to RS garment. Machine stitch along fitting line. Press seam open, then press towards the binding (see Figure 123).

Turn binding to WS. Fold under free edge of strip 5 mm. Bring the fold over to stitching line. Tack into position. Slip hem neatly. No stitches should show on the RS. Press lightly taking care not to crease the binding (see Figure 124).

Binding curved edges

The binding must be eased on to an outward curve to allow sufficient fabric to enable the binding to lie flat (see Figure 125).

The binding must be stretched on to an inner curve to avoid creases forming and the binding twisting (see Figure 126).

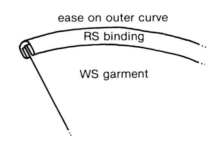

Figure 125

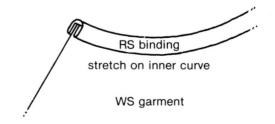

Figure 126

chapter 14

Collars

After reading this chapter you will be able to:

1   Recognize collar types.

2   Make and attach the different types of collars.

Most seasons see collars in fashion in some form or other. A collar can add interest to the basic dress style. The use of contrast in texture, colour or decorative finishes to a collar can bring individuality to a garment.

Types and styles (Figure 127)

Flat collar Peter Pan. Used on dresses. Usually on children's wear.

Straight collar Sits close to the neckline, used on dresses, blouses, jackets. Made with rever or neck line fastening.

Stand collar Mandarin. Stands up at the neck line. Used on dresses, blouses.

Shawl collar The undercollar is cut in one with the front bodice extending to the CB. Rolls back to form a soft line. Used on dresses, jackets, coats.

Polo collar Rolls back to neck line. Used on dresses, blouses.

Collar construction points

Neck line the line to which the inner edge of the collar is stitched

Style line the shape of the outer edge of the collar

Break line the crease line which turns the collar back to form a rever

Roll line the point at which the collar turns down

When making up and attaching collars, accuracy is essential to enable the collar to sit correctly. As a focal point of a garment, a collar that fits badly is very obvious.

The neck line curve is off the straight of grain and is liable to stretch. To prevent stretching, stay stitch the neck line by machine stitching 5 mm from the edge of the cutting line.

Neck line shapes and collar styles vary, but in construction the processes are basically the same.

Collars are interfaced on the underside to give firmness and support. The polo or roll collar cut on the cross-grain of the fabric is not interfaced as it needs a soft roll which cross-cutting allows it to do. Straight collars sitting close to the neck line with a definite roll line need to be cut in two pieces varying slightly in size. The undercollar is cut 3 mm smaller all round than the top collar.

Making a collar

Cut accurately, transfer markings. It is essential to mark clearly the following points:

centre back
centre front
shoulder point

Attach interfacing to WS of undercollar. Placing RSS together, tack and machine stitch outer edge of collar leaving neck edge free. Grade seam allowance by trimming down to different widths to reduce bulk. Press seam open using point of iron (see Figure 128).

Rounded collar

After grading seam allowance, notch seam allowance along the rounded edge (see Figure 129a).

straight   stand   shawl   polo

flat

Figure 127

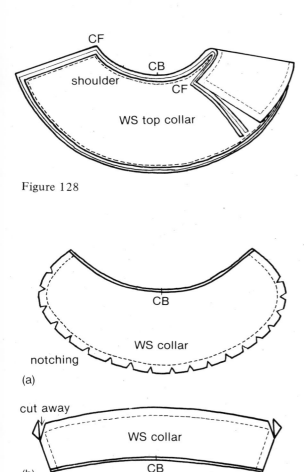

Figure 128

Figure 129

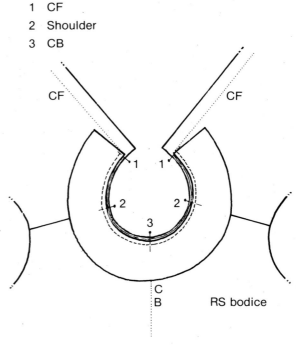

1 CF
2 Shoulder
3 CB

Figure 130

Methods of finishing

The neck edge must be neatened when the collar has been attached. There are various ways to do this.

Front and back facings

Make up collar. Tack to neck edge. Machine stitch front and back facings at shoulders. Neaten outer edge of facing. Place RS facing to RS collar. Tack and machine stitch facing to neck line matching at centre points and shoulder points.

Grade seam allowance, and clip into seam allowance at 1.5 cm intervals. Press seam open. Turn facing to WS of garment. Press. Secure facing with small stitches at shoulder seams (see Figure 131).

Crosswise facing

Make up collar. Tack to neck edge. Trim neck edge seam to 5 mm. Cut crosswise strip 4 cm wide × collar length + 2 cm seam allowance. Machine stitch

Straight collar

After grading seam allowance, cut across pointed corner diagonally to make a good point to the collar (see Figure 129b).

Turn collar to RS. The seam must sit exactly on the outer edge of the collar. The undercollar must not show when the garment is being worn. Press collar carefully.

Attaching collar

Pin collar to neck edge, placing pins at the five balance points. Ease collar to fit neck edge. Tack in place (see Figure 130).

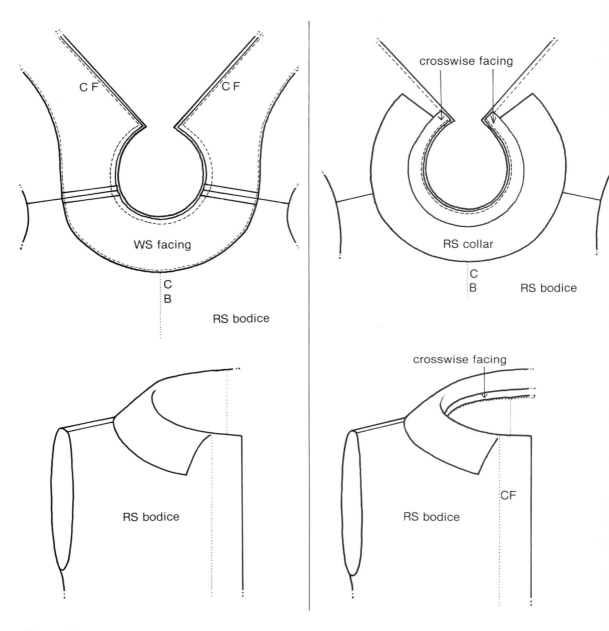

Figure 131

Figure 132

strip to collar, easing the strip so that it does not pull too tightly. Turn in free edge of strip; turn in 1 cm seam allowance at each end of strip. Tack down strip to WS neck line so that it lies flat (see Figure 132). Hem. Press.

Front facing only

Attach front facing to bodice placing RSS together, stitching along neck edge to collar fitting point only. Clip. Press. Turn facing to WS. Make up collar.

Placing RS collar to WS bodice, pin and tack top collar to neck edge, matching balance marks.

Machine stitch top collar and facing to bodice. Trim seam allowance. Clip. Press seam open, then press seam allowance upwards towards collar. Bring undercollar down to neck edge on RS of bodice, enclosing seam allowance inside collar. Tack and hem undercollar to neck line (see Figure 133).

No facing

Polo collar may be attached to neck edge without a facing. Make up collar. Placing RS collar to RS bodice; tack collar to neck edge, easing the collar to match up at centre points and shoulder point.

Machine stitch. Press seam open, then press seam allowance upwards to collar. Fold undercollar to neck edge (see Figure 134). Tack and hem into place. Press.

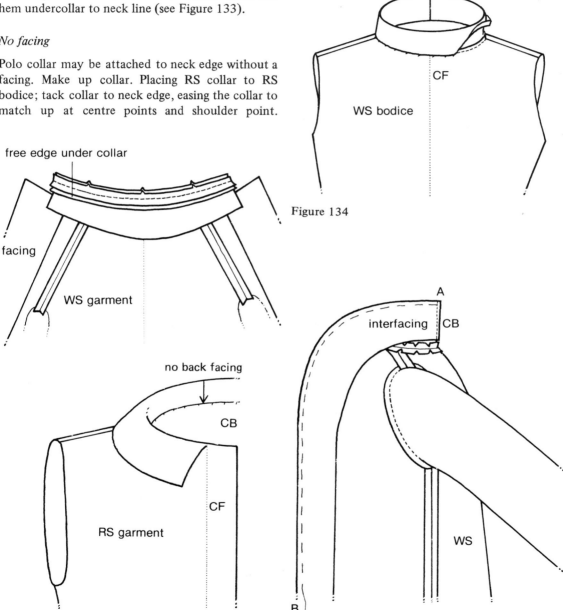

free edge under collar

facing

WS garment

Figure 134

CF

WS bodice

no back facing

CB

CF

RS garment

Figure 133

A

interfacing CB

WS

B

Figure 135

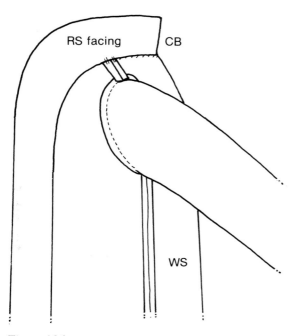

RS facing   CB

WS

Figure 136

Shawl collar

The undercollar and front bodice are cut in one piece. Attach interfacing to undercollar and front bodice. Machine stitch CB of undercollar. Press seam open. Machine stitch back neck to undercollar. Press seam open.

Clip into corners. Tack and machine stitch back neck facing to top collar. Press seam open. Tack collar to under collar and front bodice along the outer edge (see Figure 135, A–B). Machine stitch. Press open seam allowance. Grade and trim seam allowance. Clip. Turn top collar to WS of garment. Press. Hand stitch seams at back neck together to hold collar in position. Tack facing down at shoulder seam (see Figure 136).

Sleeves

After reading this chapter you will be able to:

1 Recognize sleeve shapes.

2 Set in a sleeve.

3 Choose and apply a sleeve edge finish.

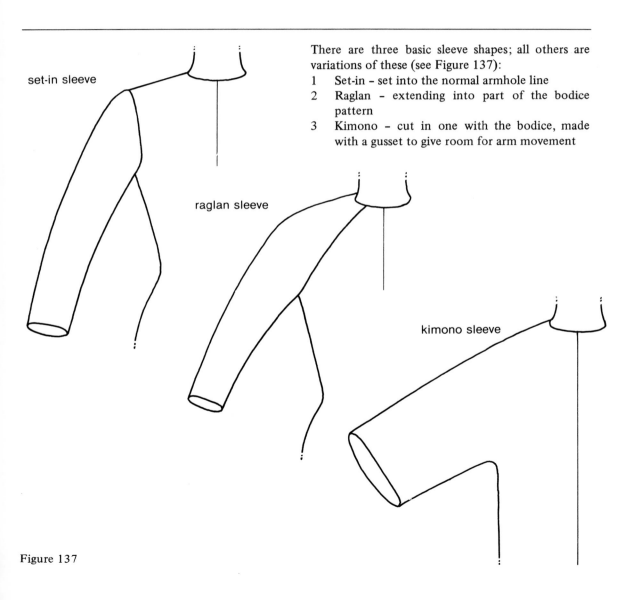

set-in sleeve

raglan sleeve

kimono sleeve

There are three basic sleeve shapes; all others are variations of these (see Figure 137):

1 Set-in – set into the normal armhole line

2 Raglan – extending into part of the bodice pattern

3 Kimono – cut in one with the bodice, made with a gusset to give room for arm movement

Figure 137

Set-in sleeve

The sleeve must be made up, seams neatened, the cuff (if any) attached before setting into the armhole.

The measurement of the sleeve-head is always greater than the armhole measurement (approximately 4 cm). The sleeve must be eased into the armhole.

Pin sleeve into armhole placing the pins at right angles to the fitting line. Match at notches, underarm seams and shoulder point. By manipulating the sleeve between the thumb and forefinger, distribute the ease evenly, pinning to secure (see Figure 138).

Tack sleeve into armhole using short stitches to hold the eased sleeve in position and to prevent it slipping and gathers forming when the sleeve is being machine stitched. Commencing at underarm

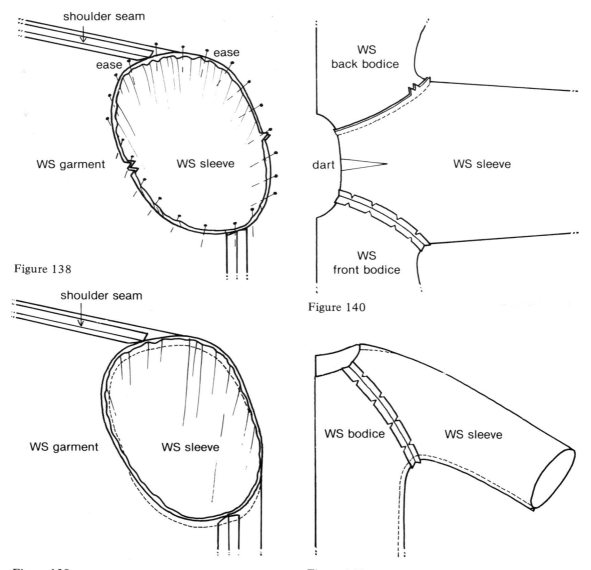

Figure 138

Figure 139

Figure 140

Figure 141

seam, machine stitch the sleeve into the armhole (see Figure 139). Trim seams. Neaten raw edges together. Press seam towards sleeve.

Raglan sleeve

Machine stitch dart at shoulder point. Press open. Placing RS together, tack and machine stitch front and back sleeves to front and back bodices,

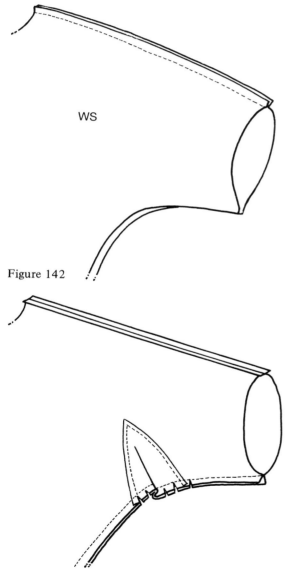

Figure 142

Figure 143

matching notches (see Figure 140). Clip into curved seam lines. Press seams open.

The side seam and underarm seams are machine stitched in one operation, matching seams at underarm point (see Figure 141). Press seams open.

Kimono sleeve

For gusset insertion see Chapter 20. Tack and machine stitch shoulder and upper sleeve seams (see Figure 142). Press open.

Machine stitch underarm and side seams (see Figure 143). Clip curved seams. Press open.

Cuffs and sleeve edge finishes

As with everything in fashion, sleeve finishes vary with current trends. The following classic finishes are used constantly in some form or other.

Turn back cuff

With RSS facing, machine stitch ends of cuff. Press seam open. Pin RS cuff to WS sleeve edge. Machine stitch (see Figure 144).

Press seam towards cuff. Turn in seam allowances on free edge of cuff. Slip stitch to seam on RS of sleeve (see Figure 145).

Press cuff towards sleeve. Catch with two or three stitches at sleeve seam (see Figure 146).

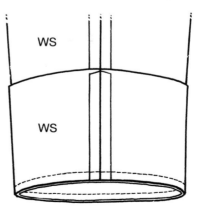

Figure 144

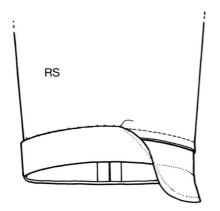

Figure 145

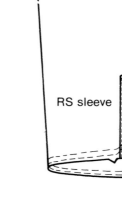

Figure 148

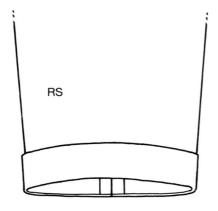

Figure 146

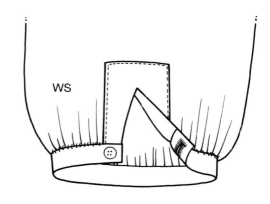

Figure 149

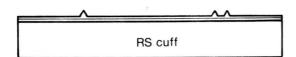

Figure 147

Open cuff

Fold cuff lengthwise, attach interfacing, machine stitch ends. Trim seams, press, turn to RS (see Figure 147). Press.

Gather lower edge of sleeve (see Figure 148). Pin, tack and machine stitch cuff to sleeve, matching notches and adjusting the gathers evenly.

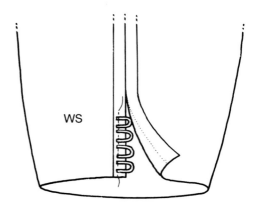

Figure 150

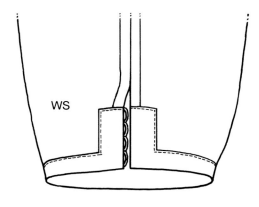

Figure 151

Turn under free edge of cuff, and slip stitch to seam on WS. Work buttonhole, sew on button (see Figure 149).

Rouleau loop closure

Machine stitch sleeve seam to within 8 cm of sleeve edge. Press open. Make loops (see Chapter 12). Cut into short lengths. Tack loops to back edge of sleeve opening (see Figure 150).

Placing RSS together, neaten opening and sleeve edge with facing (see Figure 151). Sew buttons to front edge of opening.

chapter 16

Interfacings and linings

After reading this chapter you will be able to:

1 Recognize when and where to use interfacings.

2 Select the correct type of interfacing for the fabric being worked.

3 Select interlinings and linings.

4 Attach linings to garments.

Interfacings are used to give firmness and shape to a garment. They are used between the main garment pieces and the facings. Neck lines, collars, cuffs and pocket flaps are interfaced to reinforce and support them. There are different types and weights of interfacings, and it is important to select the correct interfacing for the fabric weight and content.

Non-woven interfacings do not have a 'straight of grain'; therefore the pattern pieces can be cut in any direction. Woven interfacings must be cut on the same grain as the garment pieces. Iron-on interfacings give firm support to a fabric. Always test on a small piece of fabric before using on the garment pieces to make sure that the correct firmness required has been established. A stretchable interfacing must be used on all knitted fabrics to keep the natural stretch and characteristics of such fabrics. Figure 152 is a guide to the choice of interfacings for the fabric being worked.

Interlinings are placed between the garment and the lining to give warmth and firmness. Use the lining pattern pieces for cutting out. The interlining is constructed separately. Machine stitch the shoulder seams together and the side seams together, then catch-stitch the interlining to the edge of the facings (see Figure 153).

Linings and underlinings

Both lining and underlining give a finished garment more warmth, a smooth line over the figure and a professional inside finish. They are used differently in the construction of the garment.

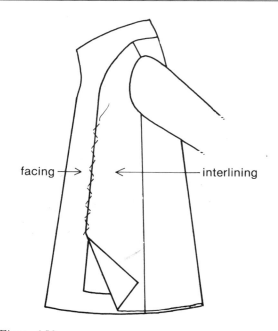

facing → ← interlining

Figure 153

Underlining or mounting

The garment is assembled treating the two layers (that is, top fabric and lining) as one fabric, following the instructions for making up the garment. This method of lining gives the support needed when working with loosely woven fabrics, sheers and lace, depending upon the style of the garment and the required 'hang'.

Figure 152   *Interfacing guide chart*

Type	Colour	Description	Width	Care	Usage
Lawn	White, assorted colours	Fine light-weight woven cotton	91 cm	Washable	Facings, collars, cuffs in fine light-weight fabrics
Organdie	White, black	Sheer light-weight woven cotton	112 cm	Washable	To add crispness to facings, collars, cuffs in fine light-weight fabrics
Taffetta	Assorted colours	Woven medium-crisp light-weight rayon	91 cm	Dry clean	Light-weight wool and mixture fabrics
Hair canvas	Natural	Woven medium-weight rayon/hair, also iron-on type	82 cm	Dry clean	Suits and coats in light and medium-weight fabrics
Canvas	Natural, black, grey, white	Woven linen	82 cm	Dry clean	Light-weight tailoring
French canvas	White, black	Woven linen, also iron-on type	61 cm	Dry clean	Collars in light-weight tailoring
Bonded	White, black, grey	Non-woven light-weight, also iron-on light-weight	81 cm	Washable	Soft materials, light-weight cottons, synthetics
Bonded	White, black	Non-woven medium-weight, also iron-on medium-weight	81 cm	Washable	Use for a soft line on light-weight woollens and synthetics
Bonded	White	Non-woven heavy-weight, also iron-on heavy-weight	81 cm	Washable, dry clean	Heavy-weight cottons and rayons
Bonded	White	Non-woven transparent iron-on	81 cm	Washable, dry clean	Light-weight and sheer fabrics
Bonded	White	Non-woven light-weight stretchable iron-on	81 cm	Washable, dry clean	Use on light and medium-weight knitted fabrics
Bonded webbing	White	Non-woven fusible	91 cm, also 3 cm	Washable, dry clean	Bonds fabrics together, used on hems, buttonholes
Woven iron-on	White, black	Woven light-weight iron-on	81 cm	Washable, dry clean	Light-weight materials, cottons, synthetics
Bonded waistband	White, cream	Non-woven heavy-weight	3 cm	Washable, dry clean	Waistbands, belts
Bonded	Cream	Non-woven light-weight stretchable iron-on	81 cm	Washable, dry clean	Use on needlecord

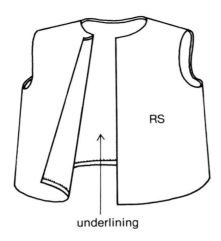

Figure 154

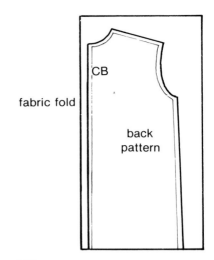

Figure 155

The main sections of a garment are underlined. To avoid bulk at the armhole, it is better to leave the sleeve without an underlining. The hem is turned up and attached to the underlining only. This prevents a ridge forming on the RS of the garment (see Figure 154).

Loose lining

The choice of a suitable lining is important. It must be smooth and comfortable and must be the correct weight to line up with the top fabric. A toning or contrasting shade may be used depending upon the effect required. It must also launder in the same way.

The entire garment may be lined or part of the garment, for example, the back only of a straight skirt in order to help control stretching of the top fabric.

Linings are usually cut from the same pattern pieces as the garment. Jacket and coat linings are cut 2 cm wider at the CB to allow a small pleat arrangement to give added ease to the lining (see Figure 155).

Making

Transfer all pattern markings to the lining pieces. Make up the lining in the same way that the

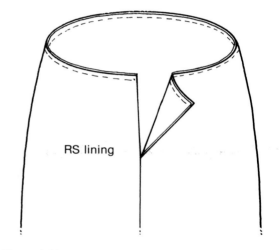

Figure 156

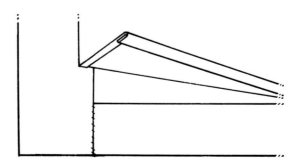

Figure 157

garment was made up. In skirts and trousers the made-up lining is tacked to the waist line before the waistband is attached (see Figure 156).

The same allowance on the lining is turned under along the placket opening edges and slip-stitched in place (see Figure 157). Finish the lining hem 2 cm shorter than the garment hem line.

To line a dress completely, the lining is attached by hand along the zipper tape or to the edge of the facing depending upon the type of opening. The bodice and sleeve linings are attached along the armhole line. The sleeve edge of the lining is slip-stitched over the hem of the sleeve of the garment.

Some fabric suggestions for interlinings are:

Fusible fleece
Sheet wadding
For linings suggested materials include:
Aluminium backed satin*
Crêpe-de-chine
Japsilk
Satin
Taffetta
Tricel

Note: This lining fabric has been treated with an aluminium coating to give it good insulation. Used in coats and raincoats, it gives more warmth to the garment.

chapter 17

Skirt waist finishes

After reading this chapter you will be able to:

1 Choose a waistband suitable for the style and fabric being worked.

2 Apply the waistband correctly.

The importance of a good finish to the waist line of a skirt or trousers cannot be over-emphasized as the garment hangs from this point on the figure. It must be comfortable and should fit snugly at the natural waist line whatever finish is decided upon.

Fabric waistband

A classic finish, usually 2.5–4 cm wide, made with an underlap to give a neat closing detail.

Cut on lengthwise grain of fabric. *Size* – waist measurement + seam allowances + underlap 4 cm × twice width of finished band + seam allowances.

The waistband should be interfaced to give a firm finish and to prevent the band stretching.

Making and attaching waistband

Mark centre points on skirt waist edge. Mark centre points, side seams on skirt waistband. Attach interfacing to band (see Figure 158).

Fold band lengthwise RS together. Machine stitch both ends. On underlap clip to turn band easily and to allow seam allowances to lie flat. Turn band to RS (see Figure 159). Press.

Place RS band to RS skirt matching up at CB, CF and SS to give correct balance. Pin, tack and machine stitch one edge of band leaving the other edge free. Ease the skirt on to the band. Remove tacking, trim seam allowance to avoid bulk inside the band (see Figure 160). Press.

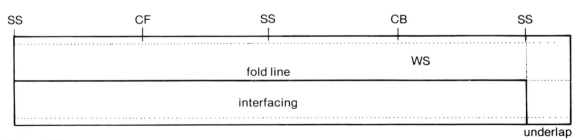

Figure 158

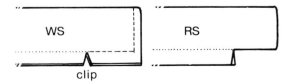

Figure 159

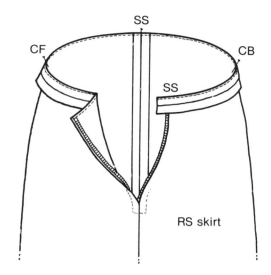

Figure 160

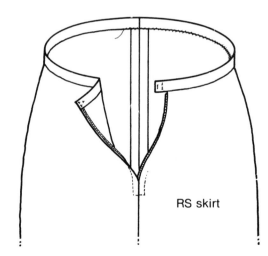

Figure 161

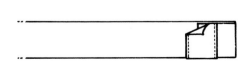

Figure 162

Turn under seam allowance of free edge of band. Place fold along stitching line on WS. Slip stitch band neatly. Press. Finish with hooks and eyes on underlap (see Figure 161).

Petersham – tailored finish

The petersham finish at the skirt waist eliminates bulk and gives a smooth, firm line. The petersham must be pre-shrunk. One made of synthetic yarn will not shrink. Straight or pre-shaped petersham may be used. *Size* – waist measurement + 2 cm.

Attaching to skirt

Turn under 1 cm at each end of petersham. Attach a small piece of seam binding over raw edges to neaten. Machine stitch in place (see Figure 162).

Tack one edge of petersham to WS waist seam line. Distribute ease evenly so that the correct balance of the skirt is maintained. Tack seam binding to petersham; centre binding over raw edge of skirt waist. Machine stitch both edges of binding (see Figure 163, A–B).

Turn upper edge of skirt at waist line to WS, setting the petersham to the inside of the skirt. Press. Attach hooks and eyes at skirt opening.

Faced waist line

A shaped band to form a facing gives a neat finish to skirts hanging from just below the natural waist line. Light-weight interfacing gives enough support to keep the shape of the facing.

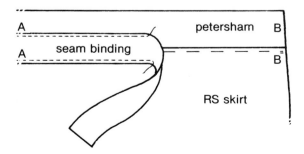

Figure 163

Cutting

Follow the natural curve of the waist line. *Size* –
waist measurement + seam allowance tapering out
according to side seam line. *Depth* – 5–7 cm. Cut
interfacing to the same size (see Figure 164).

Tack and machine stitch RS facing to RS skirt.
Trim seam allowances. Press. Turn facing to WS
skirt. Neaten loose edge of facing. Secure at side
seams and at skirt opening. Finish with hooks and
eyes (see Figure 165).

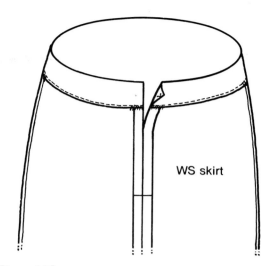

WS skirt

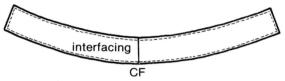

interfacing

CF

Figure 164   Figure 165

chapter 18

Hems

After reading this chapter your will be able to:

1 Choose the correct hem finish for the style of garment and fabric being worked.

2 Level, mark and neaten a hem line.

The purpose of the hem is to add weight to the edge of the garment to help it hang properly. The fabric and the style will determine the type of hem used. Current fashion plays an important part in the skirt length, but it is essential that the correct hem is used and that it has a professional finish.

All final adjustments must be made before the hem is marked. Allow the garment to hang for at least twelve hours before marking the hem line. The correct underwear, shoes and belt, if any, must be worn when the hem is being prepared.

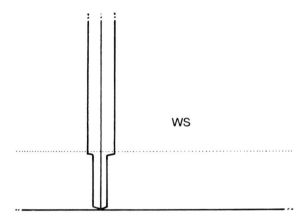

Figure 166

Levelling

The preparation of the hem process is the same for all fabrics and styles. The person being fitted must stand straight and naturally. Mark along the complete circumference of the hem every 7.5 cm.

Marking

a *Metre stick* Place firmly on the ground and measure accurately to length required, placing a pin at regular intervals along the hem line.

b *Chalk marker* A commercial marker available for use with powder chalk, giving a series of chalk marks along the required hem line.

c *Pin-it marker* Similar to b for using with pins. The marker snaps the pin in position, transferring it to the fabric along the required hem line.

Trim seam allowances to marked line to avoid bulk inside the hem (see Figure 166).

Apart from circle hems, which are narrow (3 mm–1.5 cm) and machine stitched or rolled, all hems are hand finished.

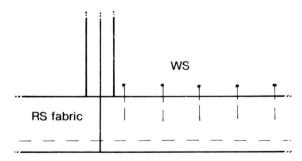

Figure 167

Fold the hem along the marked line. Pin in place with the pins at right angles to hold it firmly in position making the hem uniform in width (see Figure 167).

Tack hem 5 mm above the fold line. This will secure the hem while working.

Neatening

The type of neatening chosen depends upon the fabric being worked. The average hem depth is 5–7 cm.

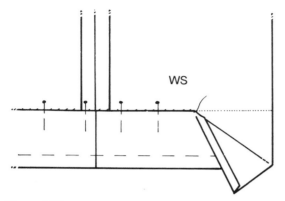

Figure 168

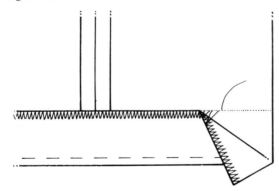

Figure 169

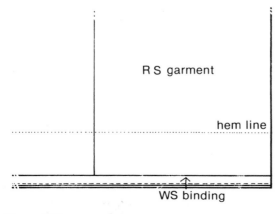

R S garment

hem line

WS binding

Figure 170

Creased-edge finish

Fold under 5 mm for first turning. Tack in place. Slip hem to garment. The creased line can be given an edge-stitched finish before slip hemming to garment. Use on light-weight fabrics (see Figure 168).

Overlock/swing needle finish

A neatening stitch to prevent the raw edges fraying. Worked on any sewing machine with swing needle attachment. Use on light to medium-weight fabrics before slip hemming to garment (see Figure 169).

Bound hem

The cut edge is encased in a crosswise binding. Machine stitch crosswise strip 2.5 cm wide to lower edge of hem placing RSS together. Stretch the strip slightly to avoid creasing. Turn strip to wrong side to form binding edge. Tack. Press, slip hem to garment. Use on thick fabrics and loosely woven fabrics (see Figures 170 and 171).

Double hem

Use on fine and semi-transparent fabrics to prevent raw edge showing through the hem to the right side. The first fold in the fabric must be as deep as the second fold. Use the creased edge finish (see Figure 172).

Pleats at hem

Clip into the seam allowance at top of hem. Press seam open within the fold of the hem. Neaten, slip

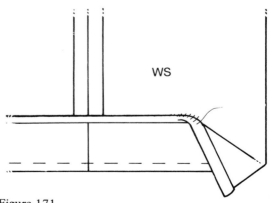

WS

Figure 171

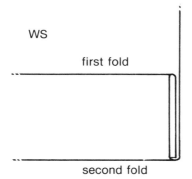

WS

first fold

second fold

Figure 172

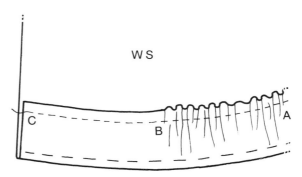

W S

C

B

A

Figure 175

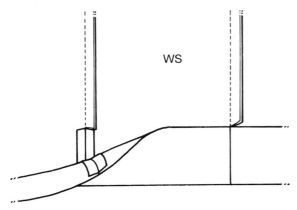

WS

Figure 173

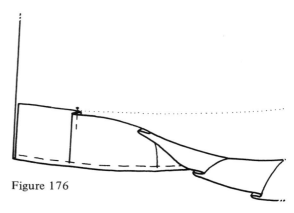

Figure 176

finger. Slip hem by taking a single thread for each stitch. The roll must be no more than 3 mm deep (see Figure 174).

A special foot attachment is available with most sewing machines to do this operation more speedily.

Reducing fullness at hems

Wool fabrics will respond to shrinking so that any surplus fabric can be removed by using heat and moisture. Run a gathering thread along raw edge of hem, and draw up the thread for required amount. Work on single fabric, applying a wet pressing cloth to the gathered area (see Figure 175, A–B).

Allow the hot iron to steam out surplus fabric (see Figure 175, B–C). Do not press too heavily. Work along the hem line until all surplus fabric is removed.

For light-weight fabrics that will not respond to shrinking, place narrow tapering folds at regular intervals until all the surplus fabric is folded out and the hem lies flat (see Figure 176).

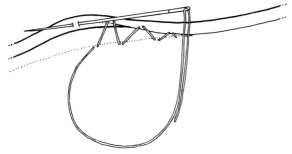

Figure 174

hem to garment, re-press the pleat to one side (see Figure 173).

Rolled hem

This gives a delicate finish to sheer fabrics. For hand finish, roll the edge between thumb and fore-

Figure 177

chapter 19

Pockets

After reading this chapter you will be able to:

1   Recognize different pocket types.

2   Determine the size and positioning of pockets.

3   Construct and apply pockets into a garment.

Pockets are used in dressmaking for decorative use and also as a functional part of the garment. They are separated into two types, those that are placed on to the garment as a patch, and those that are set into a seam or into a slash in the fabric.

Success depends upon a few important rules.

1   Mark the pocket positions accurately.
2   Keep the corners and the edges of the pocket crisp.
3   Pull the pocket bag through gently, clipping right into the corners.
4   Keep welts and flaps balanced by accurate measuring of the finished work.
5   Slip stitch welts invisibly to the garment.
6   Never overpress or cause shine and ridges on the pocket.

Pocket sizes and positions

The size of a pocket depends upon whether it is for use or for decoration. It must tie in with the style of the garment and should be positioned to give balance.

A breast pocket placed on the bodice front measures 7.5-10 cm wide.

Hip pockets must be so placed that they are comfortable to use. Hip pockets must be the breadth of the hand plus allowance for movement. The average size is 12-15 cm wide.

For some uses of pockets in design, see Figure 177.

Pocket types

Patch pocket

The basic shape of a patch pocket is decided by the position of the pocket and the width required. Many different styles and shapes can be developed from a basic square whether small or large.

Square patch pocket

Mark position of pocket on garment. Turn in 5 mm on upper edge of pocket. Machine stitch (see Figure 178).

Make a second fold along upper edge of pocket RSS together. Machine stitch depth of fold at both sides of pocket. Clip seam allowances (see Figure 179).

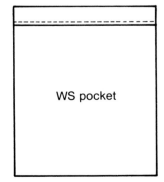

WS pocket

Figure 178

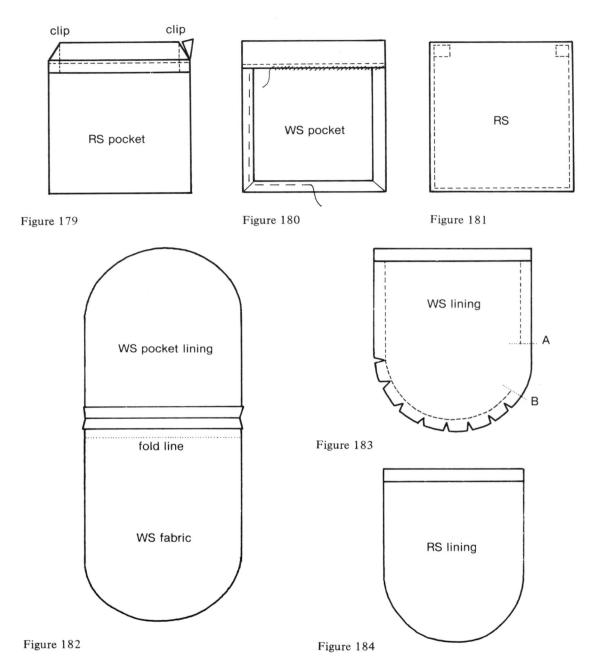

Figure 179

Figure 180

Figure 181

Figure 182

Figure 183

Figure 184

Turn hem, press, slip stitch along fold line to WS of pocket (see Figure 180).

Turn in seam allowance. Tack pocket to garment. Top stitch pocket along outer edge, strengthening the corners of the upper edge with additional stitching as shown in Figure 181.

Curved patch pocket – lined
Join lining to pocket RSS together. Press seam open (see Figure 182). Fold pocket RSS together along fold line. Machine stitch along fitting line leaving an opening in the seam, A–B (see Figure 183). Notch along curved edge. Turn pocket to RS. Press.

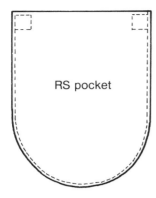

Figure 185

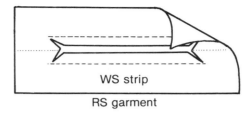

Figure 186

Tack pocket to garment. Top stitch along outer edge, strengthening the corners of the upper edge with additional stitching (see Figure 185).

Bound pocket

The method of making a bound pocket is similar to that of a bound buttonhole. A piece of fusible interfacing applied to the back (WS) of the pocket line gives a firm finish and support to the pocket.

Mark the pocket's position accurately.

For the binding, cut strip of fabric on the cross-grain – width of pocket mouth + 8 cm × 10 cm deep. Fold strip lengthwise, mark centre crease line. Tack strip to pocket position, RS strip to RS garment. Machine stitch 5 mm away from each side of crease line. Do not machine across the ends. Cut pocket mouth to within 5 mm of each end. Clip into each corner (see Figure 186).

Turn binding to inside through the opening. Work to the centre of the opening, forming an even bind on the RS of the pocket mouth and a small inverted pleat each side of the pocket mouth on the WS. Press.

For the pocket bag, piece no. 1 should be the depth of pocket + seam allowance × width of pocket binding. Piece no. 2 should be the depth of pocket + 8 cm + seam allowance × width of pocket binding.

Attach piece no. 1 to lower edge of bind on WS of garment (see Figure 187).

Attach piece no. 2 placing RSS of pocket bag together. Machine stitch to upper edge of bind (see Figure 188).

Figure 187

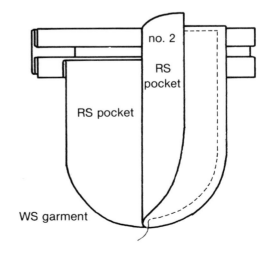

Figure 188

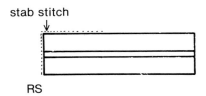

Figure 189

Machine stitch pocket bag along outer edge. Neaten. Working on RS stab stitch along binding seam line and across short ends of pocket mouth to hold the bind in place (see Figure 189). Press.

Interesting effects are achieved using fabric in various ways for a pocket binding, such as stripes and checks, as well as using various textures, such as suede, leather and velvet.

Welt pocket

The basic oblong shape of a welt may be used to give interest by varying the shape, colour and texture.

Mark pocket position accurately. Cut welt width + seam allowance × twice depth + seam allowance.

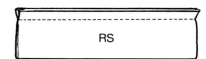

Figure 190

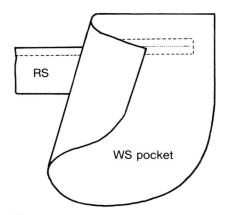

Figure 191

For example, a finished size of 12 cm × 3 cm must be cut 12 cm + 2 cm seam allowance × 6 cm + 2 cm seam allowance.

Pocket bag size – depth required × width of welt + 3 cm. Fold welt lengthwise RSS together. Interface to fold line. Machine stitch ends of welt, trim, turn to RS (see Figure 190). Press.

Tack welt to RS garment below pocket line with raw edges at the top. With RS together, tack one pocket section to garment over welt. Machine stitch 5 mm each side of marked line (see Figure 191).

Cut pocket line through garment only to within 5 mm of ends of welt. Clip into corners. Turn pocket through to WS of garment (see Figure 192).

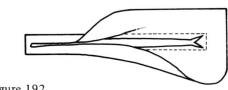

Figure 192

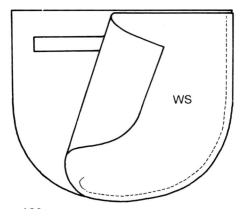

Figure 193

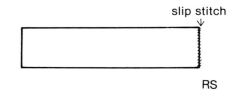

Figure 194

Attach second pocket piece. Neaten edge of pocket bag (see Figure 193).

Press welt upwards. Slip stitch edges of welt to garment (see Figure 194).

Flap pocket

Mark pocket position accurately. To make flap, cut two pieces in fabric and one piece in interfacing to size and shape required. Attach interfacing to one piece. Placing RSS together, machine stitch curved edge of flap. Notch, trim, turn to RS (see Figure 195). Press.

Tack flap above pocket line. Pocket bag size – depth × width of flap + 3 cm. Cut two. The depth of the pocket depends upon the position of the pocket on the garment; for instance, a breast pocket is smaller than a hip pocket. For a breast pocket with a flap of 9 cm × 4 cm (finished size), the pocket bag should be 8 cm (depth) × 12 cm + seam allowance.

Tack one piece of pocket to RS garment below pocket line, placing edges of flap and pocket together. Machine stitch along fitting line of flap. Allowing a space of 1.3 cm for pocket mouth, machine stitch pocket piece to within 5 mm of each

end. Cut through pocket line. Clip into corners of flap and pocket piece (see Figure 196).

Turn pocket to WS forming a bind to lower edge of pocket. Tack flap downwards on RS. Press lightly. Attach second pocket piece. Neaten. Stab stitch ends of opening to pocket to secure clipped seam allowance (see Figure 197).

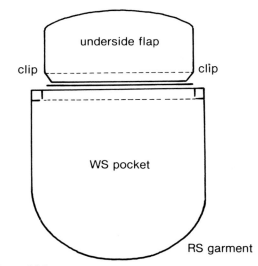

Figure 196

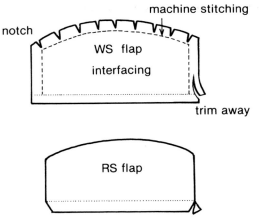

Figure 195

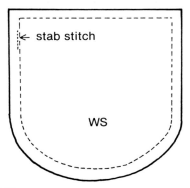

Figure 197

chapter 20

Gussets and godets

After reading this chapter you will be able to:

1   Determine the use of gussets and godets.

2   Recognize different shapes of gussets.

3   Insert a gusset and a godet.

Gussets

A gusset is a shaped piece of material inserted into a garment at the underarm point to give strength, to avoid strain and to give more freedom for arm movement while still maintaining a good fit to the sleeve. It is used with a kimono sleeve, set into a slash made in the garment at the underarm point directionally from the underarm to the neck point (see Figure 198).

Gusset shapes

Triangle gusset is used either for the front or back, or both sleeves, with the sleeve seam and bodice side seam continuing through the gussets (see Figure 199).

Diamond gusset is used as one piece for a complete sleeve (see Figure 200).

Arrow-shaped gusset is used with a short kimono sleeve to avoid strain and tearing of the garment at the underarm (see Figure 201).

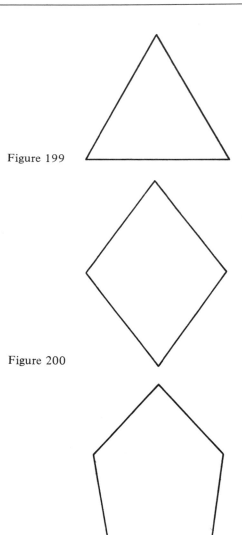

Figure 199

Figure 200

Figure 201

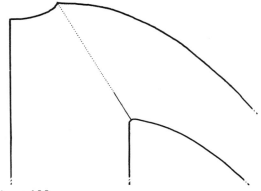

Figure 198

Strengthening the point of the slash

Cut a 5 cm square of fine fabric (lining is suitable). Place the RS of the square to the RS of the fabric at the point of the slash, matching the grain of both fabrics (see Figure 202).

Machine stitch just inside the seam line taking one stitch across the point of the slash. Cut along the slash line right into the point. Turn the square to the wrong side and press into place (see Figure 203).

Inserting triangle gusset

Placing the RSS together, pin the gusset to the slashed edges. Machine stitch along the fitting lines. Press seams open, then to one side towards the garment pieces (see Figure 204).

Inserting diamond gusset

Strengthen points of slash as illustrated in Figures 202 and 203. Join front and back bodices at side and sleeve seams. Insert gusset placing RSS together. Pin at points A, B, C, D (see Figure 205).

Machine stitch along fitting lines. Press seams open, then to one side towards garment pieces (see Figure 206).

Inserting arrow-shaped gusset

Strengthen point of slash as illustrated in Figures 202 and 203. With RSS together, pin and machine stitch the gusset to the slashed edges along fitting line. Machine stitch on RS close to seam line at point of gusset to give extra reinforcement (see Figure 207).

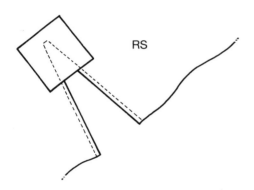

Figure 202

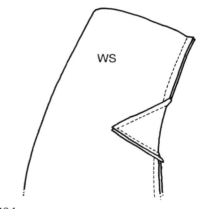

Figure 204

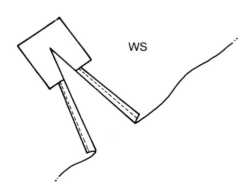

Figure 203

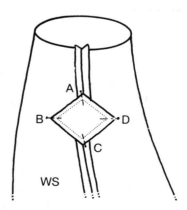

Figure 205

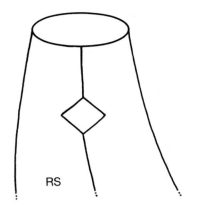

RS

Figure 206

Mark the opening for the godet. Machine stitch and slash as far as the stitched point (see Figure 209).

Pin and tack the godet into the opening, placing RSS together and matching the seam lines. Working from the base, take in the full seam allowance allowing it to taper towards the point. Machine stitch the godet into position taking one stitch across the point (see Figure 210). Press seams open, then to one side towards the main section of the garment.

For designs showing the use of godets, see Figure 211.

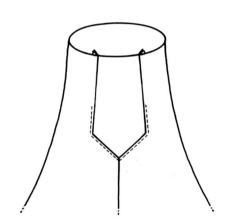

Figure 207

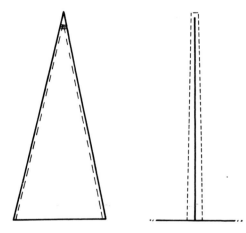

Figure 208   Figure 209

Godets

A godet is a decorative way to give movement and flare to a skirt or sleeve. It is a triangle shape inserted into a slash cut in a skirt or sleeve from the lower edge to the point decided upon for the length of the godet. The size of the godet should be three times as long as the width of the base.

Inserting a godet

Strengthen the seam edges with a row of stay stitching. Machine stitch using a standard stitch length just inside the fitting lines, taking one stitch across the top (see Figure 208).

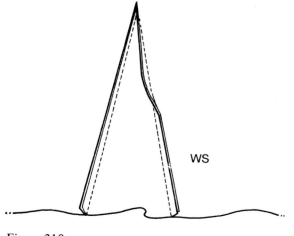

WS

Figure 210

Figure 211

chapter 21

Multiple choice questions

1 Which of these styles would flatter a figure with a small bust?
   a Princess line
   b Empire line
   c A-line
   d Dropped waist line

2 Which seam is self-neatened?
   a Piped seam
   b Open seam
   c Machine fell
   d Slot seam

3 What is basting?
   a A type of interfacing
   b Final pressing on a finished garment
   c Pressing over a hem to give shape
   d Another name for tacking

4 When applying a binding to an outer curve it should be:
   a Gathered
   b Eased
   c Stretched
   d Straight

5 The break line is the:
   a Collar stand
   b Collar crease line
   c Buttonhole position
   d Creased line of lapel

6 If sleeve pattern is too long, it should be shortened:
   a At the wrist edge
   b Above the elbow
   c Below the elbow
   d By checking elbow position, then as required

7 Styles incorporating vertical lines give a figure the appearance of being:
   a Broader
   b Flat chested
   c Taller
   d Short waisted

8 Shirring is used for:
   a Trimming seams
   b Rows of machine gathering by elastic thread
   c Grading seams in heavy-weight fabrics
   d Waistband elastic casing

9 Which sewing machine needle is the finest of these numbers?
   a 100
   b 80
   c 70
   d 90

10 A padded roller is used to:
    a Press darts
    b Press velvet
    c Avoid seam imprints
    d Flatten seams

11 What is slip tacking?
    a Diagonal tacking stitches
    b Tacking worked on the RS
    c Small running stitches
    d Long and short stitches

12   When cutting velvet you should:
      a Fold the fabric in half lengthwise
      b Fold the fabric in half widthwise
      c Place pattern pieces facing same direction
      d Cut on the underside of fabric

13   A shawl collar is:
      a Flounced
      b Cut on the cross
      c Cut in one with the bodice
      d Set on to a stand

14   What is rouleau?
      a A roll collar
      b A sleeve style
      c A tube made from crosswise strips
      d A low neck line

15   What is a French seam?
      a A double seam that looks like a tuck on the WS
      b Top stitched curved seam
      c A piped seam
      d A seam decorated with saddle stitching

16   Seams on a heavy tweed skirt are stitched with needle number:
      a 70
      b 90
      c 80
      d 100

17   Decorative pin tucking is:
      a A row of stitching appearing as a fine ridge
      b A 1 cm wide tuck
      c Three tucks grouped together
      d A 5 mm tuck stitched horizontally

18   A box pleat is:
      a An unpressed pleat
      b Two knife pleats turning away from each other
      c Two 5 cm pleats
      d An inset pleated panel

19   Synthetic sewing thread is used for stitching garments made from:
      a Needlecord
      b Wool tweed
      c Cotton print
      d Knitted polyester

20   A wire needleboard is used for:
      a Brushing wool fabrics
      b Trimming fur fabrics
      c Pressing velvet
      d Storing needles

21   What is the commercial name used for crosswise strips?
      a Russian braid
      b Tape
      c Bias binding
      d Paris binding

22   Why is it necessary to clip into the seam allow allowance?
      a To strengthen the seam
      b To enable the seam to lie flat
      c To neaten the seam
      d To let the seam out when fitting

23   Why is it necessary to match up CB, CF and SS of waistband to skirt?
      a To alter the fit
      b To give even balance to the 'hang' of the skirt
      c To attach the skirt lining
      d To attach interfacing to the band

24   Seam allowances are trimmed for the purpose of:
      a Matching up fabric pattern
      b Saving material
      c Reducing bulk within the seam
      d Easing curved seams

25   The figure best suited to wearing horizontal striped fabric is:
      a Flat chested
      b Broad hips
      c Short, petite
      d Tall, slim

Answers to multiple choice questions

1	*b*
2	*c*
3	*d*
4	*b*
5	*d*
6	*d*
7	*c*
8	*b*
9	*c*
10	*c*
11	*b*
12	*c*
13	*c*
14	*c*
15	*a*
16	*d*
17	*a*
18	*b*
19	*d*
20	*c*
21	*c*
22	*b*
23	*b*
24	*c*
25	*d*

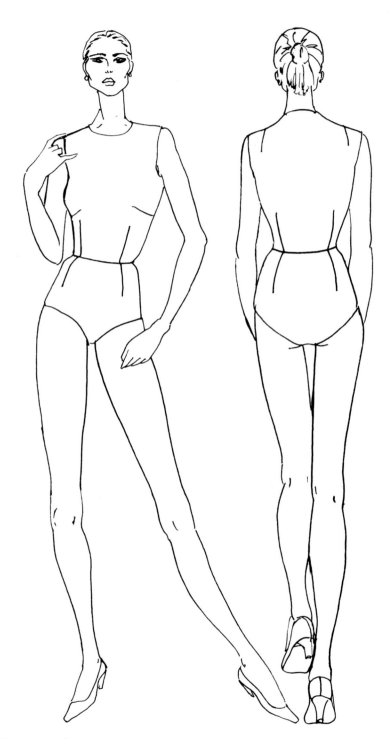

Figure 212   *Figure templates*

Index